T0082915

# Using Prayer
## *to*
# Unlock Your
# 21ˢᵗ Century
# Destiny

Prayer Saves, Works Miracles, and Blesses

DR. DOMINIC NYAABA

WESTBOW
PRESS®
A DIVISION OF THOMAS NELSON
& ZONDERVAN

Scriptures taken from the Holy Bible, New International Version®,
NIV®. Copyright © 1973, 1978, 1984, 2011 by Biblica, Inc.™ Used
by permission of Zondervan. All rights reserved worldwide. www.
zondervan.com <http://www.zondervan.com/> The "NIV" and
"New International Version" are trademarks registered in the
United States Patent and Trademark Office by Biblica, Inc.™

WestBow Press books may be ordered through booksellers or by contacting:

WestBow Press
A Division of Thomas Nelson & Zondervan
1663 Liberty Drive
Bloomington, IN 47403
www.westbowpress.com
1 (866) 928-1240

Because of the dynamic nature of the Internet, any web addresses or
links contained in this book may have changed since publication and
may no longer be valid. The views expressed in this work are solely those
of the author and do not necessarily reflect the views of the publisher,
and the publisher hereby disclaims any responsibility for them.

Any people depicted in stock imagery provided by Thinkstock are
models, and such images are being used for illustrative purposes only.
Certain stock imagery © Thinkstock.

ISBN: 978-1-9736-1723-5 (sc)
ISBN: 978-1-9736-1724-2 (e)

Print information available on the last page.

WestBow Press rev. date: 01/27/2018

# DEDICATION

*Dedicated to God the Father, God the Son, and God the Holy Spirit for Leading, guiding and protecting me in life. God has over the years inspired and encouraged me in diverse ways in every day of my life. His desire to have other believers and me as prayer warriors demonstrates the very heart and lessons of this Book. It is also dedicated to my mother Mary Abugre Nyaaba for the love and care she bestowed upon me all of my life before she departed to heaven in 2008.* I express my sincerest and profoundest gratitude to Sister Alice of St. Charles Minor Seminary of blessed Memory for her encouragement, love and care for me while I was a teenager. I dedicate this book to the Catholic Charismatic Renewal, Tamale, and University of Ghana Branches, for their spiritual training. My heart felt gratitude also goes to **Rev. Jim Adombila of Fountain Gate Chapel, Tamale, Ghana, and Rev. John Kumah Bray** of Fountain Gate Chapel, Oaugadougou, Burkina Faso for impacting so much spiritual wealth on me while I served under them as Associate pastor.

# CONTENTS

Preface..................................................................................xi

Introduction...................................................................... xiii

**CHAPTER 1** ......................................................................... 1

1. Prayer Equips You to Overcome the Amalekites of
   Your Life ...................................................................... 1
2. Prayer Ropes you into Fellowship ............................. 3
3. Prayer Against Conspiracy ........................................ 5
4. Using the imprecatory Psalms in Prayer................... 7
5. Prayer Comforts ........................................................ 9
6. Shepherd (Psalm 23: 1-5) ....................................... 11
7. God Prepares a Table Before You in the Presence of
   Your Enemies When You Pray ................................ 15
8. God Anoints You for Greater Works When You pray ........ 18
9. Anointing the Sick in Prayer (James 5:13-18)...................... 21
10. Know that Jesus is the Alpha and The Omega of your
    life when you pray ................................................... 23
11. Know that you are more than a conqueror......................... 24
12. Be Humble When You Pray ..................................... 25
13. Those Who Wait on the Lord will Renew
    Their Strength......................................................... 29
14. Eagle Christians are good trainers............................. 34
15. Eagles Never Eat Dead Meat................................... 35
16. Prayer opens Your Spiritual Eyes and Authenticates
    Your Vision.............................................................. 36

17. Prayer Rescues you from the Lions' Den (Dan 6:1-28)........38
18. A call for cooperate prayers in times of crisis ......................43
19. Prayer of Confession ................................................................45
20. Confessing the sin of nations................................................48
21. Prayer of protection................................................................49

## CHAPTER 2 ...................................................................................53

22. Making Time to Know God-The congregation ..................53
23. Making Time to Know God-The Elders..............................54
24. Prayer involves listening.......................................................55
25. Mary listened to Jesus...........................................................56
26. A prayer Saturated with Faith Moves Mountains...............57
27. Prayer and Understanding the Word of God will
    make you a Wise person......................................................60
28. Prayer, Faith and Hope ........................................................61
29. Faith has great recompense of reward (Heb. 11: 6).............63
30. Noah's Faith, Samuel and Jesus' favor. ...............................63
31. Faith is a producer of good reports (Heb. 11:2-35) .............66

## CHAPTER 3 ...................................................................................68

32. Prayer solves multiple problems...........................................68
33. Hezekiah Healed of Sickness (Isaiah 38) ...........................69
34. Jonah Prayed in the Belly of a Fish ....................................71
35. Paul and Silas Prayed ...........................................................73
36. King Asa Prayed ...................................................................75

## CHAPTER 4 ...................................................................................80

37. Prayer involves spiritual Warfare.........................................80
38. The Believer, and Spiritual Warfare
    (Ephesians 6: 10-17)............................................................81
39. Be strong in the Lord, and in the power of his might and
    Putting on the full armor of God that you may be able to
    stand against the wiles of the devil (Eph. 6:10-11) .............82
40. We do not Wrestle Against Flesh and Blood, therefore
    Take up the Full armor of God (Eph. 6:12-13) ....................83

41. Girding the Waist with truth, Putting on the breastplate of righteousness, and Proclaiming the Gospel of Peace (Eph. 6: 14-15) ............................................................87
42. The shield of faith and the Helmet of Salvation (Eph. 6:16-17) .......................................89

**CHAPTER 5** ........................................................92

43. Tithe And Offering Intelligence. ...........................92
44. Righteousness Intelligence ...................................95
45. The Intelligence Of Courage And Strength...........101
46. Prayer involves Forgiveness ...............................108
47. Forgiveness makes prayers effective .....................111

**CHAPTER 6** ........................................................113

48. How to Arise and Shine I Chronicles 4:9 ...........113
49. He refused to live in Sorrow ..............................114
50. He was honorable ..............................................115
51. He was monotheistic in prayer ...........................116
52. He cried to the lord for help ..............................118
53. Prayer will fortify you in times of trials and Temptation ....................................................119
54. Prayer will help you subdue moral conflict.........121

**CHAPTER 7** ........................................................123

55. Taming the Tongue (James 3: 1-12) ....................123
56. The tongue must be controlled because it has the power to control (V. 2-5)....................................124
57. Prayer Involves Rebuking the Enemy..................127

**CHAPTER 8** ........................................................129

58. Cultivate the Habit of Praising God ...................129
59. Understanding Praise Palms ...............................130
60. Praise God for present and everlasting providence...........132
61. Cultivate the Habit of Thanking God .................132
62. Theological implications of the Psalms of Thanksgiving 134

63. Direct Your Prayer to the Miracle Worker- Jesus Christ..135

64. Persistent prayer in Luke 18:1-8 ................................ 136

65. Attitude of the widow and the unjust judge ...................... 137

**CHAPTER 9** ................................................................ 140

66. Prayer and Spiritual Maturity ................................... 140

67. Cognitive, Relational, Volitional Faith and Spiritual
    Maturity ........................................................ 142

68. Holiness of God and Spiritual Maturity ......................... 143

69. Consequentialist and egoist theories ........................... 144

70. Utilitarianism ................................................ 145

71. Deontological ethics .......................................... 146

72. Character/ virtue ethics ...................................... 146

73. Christian worldview foundation for ethics ..................... 147

74. Motifs For Making Ethical Decision ............................ 148

75. Deliberative motif ............................................ 148

76. Prescriptive motif ............................................ 149

77. Relational motif .............................................. 150

78. Bible in ethical decisions .................................... 150

**CHAPTER 10** ............................................................... 152

79. Prayer and Heart Disease Statistics ........................... 152

80. Women and Heart Disease ....................................... 153

81. Overweight/Obesity ............................................ 154

82. High Blood Pressure ........................................... 155

83. High Cholesterol .............................................. 155

84. Jesus Prevented Me From Dying Of Heart Attack ............ 157

Conclusion .................................................................. 159

Biography of Dominic Adua A. Nyaaba, Ph.D. ................... 160

Academic Resume/ Curriculum Vitae .......................... 163

Bibliography ................................................................ 179

# PREFACE

This book lays the foundation stone for unearthing your destiny through prayer. Prayer is the Life-wire by which you Triumph in life. This book will give you the needed spiritual strength to subdue and triumph over every dicey situation in your life. Prayer has the ability to extricate you from the jaws of danger and death. Seemingly impossible financial problems are resolved by means of prayer. Prayer accompanied by supernatural anointing breaks the yoke of bondage and delivers you from the entangled web of Satan. Prayer backed by supernatural anointing cures every disease. Prayer back by supernatural anointing gives you success in all your endeavors. Anointing coupled with prayer will make you an invincible 21$^{st}$ century leader. Prayer will make you unconquerable in every facet of your life. Prayer gives you hope and makes you to recognize that the chief shepherd-Jesus would never abandon you. Prayer gives you the might you need to overcome the Amalekites and the Philistines of your life. Prayer provides divine assistance against conspiracy. Prayer annihilates rulers, authorities, and powers of the dark world and against spiritual forces of evil in the heavenly realms. Prayer gives you the anointing of David and the might of Samson to asphyxiate the Philistines and every enemy of your life. Prayer provokes divine assistance making you to possess the Land in business, in education, in politics, in your community, and in your society.

Prayer is action in faith. Abraham, Noah, Enoch, Jacob, Samson, Deborah, Esther, Roth, Naomi, Jehoshaphat, Asah, Josiah, Hezekiah, and David acted in Faith and authenticated their calling. Prayer solves multiple problems. King Hezekiah and King Jehoshaphat overcame multitudes of problems by provoking divine assistance. Peter, John, James, Matthew, Luke, Mark, Joseph, the foster father of Jesus, Paul, and his co-missionaries strangulated the enemy via Christocentric prayers. Prayer assures you of your career and exudes the abundant blessings of God on every facet of your life. You will experience the love, protection, comfort, and hope of God as you pray. Reading this Magnus opus will make you lay hold of your destiny and prosperity in the 21st century.

Jesus prayed on numerous occasions before calling his apostles. He prayed for nations, kingdoms and territories. He prayed for the apostles, for his disciples, and for himself. Prayer centered on Jesus Christ illuminates your mind and eyes so that you would be able to call the right leaders to assist you. Prayer fills your kneading troth and brings you prosperity if you believe in Jesus. Prayer heals the mentally deranged, and the physically incapacitated. Those suffering from cardio-vascular diseases, Diabetes, High blood Cholesterol, obesity, overweight, dropsy, leprosy, seizers or epileptics are delivered from the grip of Satan via Christocentric prayers . Prayer resurrects the dead. Jesus prayed and resurrected Lazarus and the son of the woman of Nain. Prayer has the potency of delivering you and oozing out the manifold blessings of God on you. Prayer will lay the bedrock of success for your business, and endeavors. It is a divine means by which you accomplish your goals, purposes, visions and dreams of the 21st century.

# INTRODUCTION

In this masterpiece, I endeavor to give a flawless Old and New Testaments biblical exegesis and exposition of selected passages. The book deals with critical analysis of every scene, episode and each historical implication of God's relationship with the people of Israel and the New Testament Church as they used prayer to relate with God and to solve seemingly impossible problems.

To facilitate the fullest comprehension of this magnum opus, I classify the work into ten major chapters. The first two components critically examine the biblical principles embedded in the Pentateuch, historical books and some New Testament texts. This segment examines how Moses and the people of Yahweh used prayer to vanquish the Amalekites in the sweltering desert as they sojourned to the Promised Land. It also dilates on the importance of anointing in the ministry of the pastor, Bishop or leader. Under this subdivision, I also give an in-depth elucidation on the nature of a good shepherd, waiting on the Lord and the method of reenergizing one's spiritual fervor as that of an eagle. The section also expatiates on a host of biblical texts where Christocentric people solved dicey problems via prayer in both the Old and New Testaments.

In the Second constituent, that is from chapter three through four, I unravel the spiritual wealth enshrined in life of King Hezekiah, Jonah and spiritual warfare in Ephesians 6:10-17. This segment consists of *The History of Israel's Nationhood of Judah, Conquest of the Assyrian Invasion, and unfathomable prosperity of the kingdom under Hezekiah.* I also dedicate an enormous space to the explanation of the prayer of Paul and Silas in Acts 16. The leadership style of king Asa as he prayed with the people of Judah and annihilated the cushites is also accentuated.

Concerning the Third subdivision, that is from chapter five through six, I expound on the types of intelligence, placing high premium on *Tithe and offering intelligence, righteousness intelligence, courage and strength intelligence. Un-forgiveness, which is a cankerworm in the 21st century is also given a high premium. Much is penned on the fruitfulness of forgiveness, and how to arise and shine.*

In shaping the Fourth part of the Book, I provide a comprehensive evaluation of James 3: 1-12. The text dilates on the need for all believers to tame their tongues in this perilous world (*kosmos*). The portion also accentuates the indispensable role of praise and thanksgiving psalms in the Israelite community. Praise and thanksgiving are a barometer by which we receive magnitude proportions of God's blessings.

The last section, that is from chapter nine through ten deals with prayer and spiritual maturity as we struggle to make educative, informative, and godly centered decisions. Moral theories are elucidated to help readers make decisions that are heavenly, and thus exude material blessings on them. Finally, the book delves into Prayer and Heart Disease Statistics, Women and Heart Disease, Overweight/obesity, High Blood Pressure, High Cholesterol, and Testimony-how Jesus saved me from Dying of Heart Attack. Jesus, the master physician is capable of healing you of every cardiovascular disease. My curriculum Vitae and Biography are at the tail end.

# CHAPTER 1

## PRAYER EQUIPS YOU TO OVERCOME THE AMALEKITES OF YOUR LIFE

Prayer gives you the energy, vigor, power, determination, zeal and resilience to overcome the undesirable Amalekites in your life. The Amalekites were the progeny of Amalek, the grandson of Esau, the elder brother of Jacob (Gen 36: 16). They vehemently provoked unholy war against the Israelites as they were journeying in the desert to the Promised Land. They attacked Israel at the time they were so weary and worn out. The Amalekites were well-trained foot army that knew how to assault their enemy in times of physical warfare. As the Israelites journeyed to the Promised Land, the Amalekites vowed to annihilate them with their military prowess. So they were known as **the first among the nations** to wage war against God's people (Num. 24:20).

Moses being an epitome of a great leader exhibited skills that paved way for urgent response and success. They were compelled to engage in the fiercest battle in the sweltering weather of the desert. Moses and the Israelites had to fight a battle that they did not prepare for. As Moses held up his hands, the Israelites overcame the Amalekites, and as he lowered his hands, the Amalekites were winning. Therefore, Joshua, the son of Nun Held up Moses hands. He supported Moses to lift up his hands so that they could subdue and subjugate the Amalekites. The Israelites defeated them with a spectacular manifestation of God's glory. The battle favored the Israelites. They emerged out of their weariness as invincible unit of God's army.

Remember the time that the Amalekites attacked God's people. It was a period of weariness or exhaustion. Scriptures asserts that they were "weary and worn out." In order to overcome the seemingly impossible situation, they had to resort to prayer. Prayer was the surface-to-surface missile that they used to vanquish a powerful opponent. Even in times of stress, depression, earthquakes, economic recession or depression or at the time of recuperating from a sickness or a surgery, the Lord is always faithful and just to give you victory over your enemies. As years went by, the Amalekites were not only defeated, they were blotted out of the surface of the earth. According to Gen 12: 3, their memory was to be blotted out from under heaven (Num. 24:20). This promise was partially fulfilled during the time of King Saul (1Sam 15 and Hezekiah (1Chr4: 43). However, it was not until the death of Haman, the Agagite (Esther 7:10) and his descendants in (Esther 9: 7-10) that the last of the Amalekites was destroyed.

God encourages you to become a prayer warrior so that you will be thoroughly equipped to fight every spiritual battle that confronts you. When you are prepared with the word of God, you are able to pray and overcome difficult problems in times of crises, and calamities. The Israelites did not only defeat the Amalekites in the sweltering weather of the wilderness, they were exterminated. The Amalekites in your life stand the greatest risk of been phased out of the surface of the earth. Your prayer carries tons and tons of spiritual ballistic missiles that are capable of overcoming every Amalekite-like situation in your life. You are not just a prayer giant; you are a recipient of God's promise as you journey to possess the land. Those who fight you, the Lord will fight them. Those who make derogatory and inflammatory remarks about you, the Lord will fight them. Those who curse you, the Lord will curse them.

Prayer would produce total victory over all your enemies. Prayer is the **Key** to success.

## PRAYER ROPES YOU INTO FELLOWSHIP

Koinoinia means fellowship. According to Webster's Ninth New Collegiate Dictionary, *fellowship* means "companionship, company, a state of being a fellow or associate, company of equals or friends or a state of being comradely or intercourse." Therefore, the word koinoinia is derived from the Greek word koinos, "common". Koinos is from the word we get "koine" which refers to the world from 332 BCE to 325 BCE. It connotes the share or degree, which one has in anything, or participation. It also stands for "living in a community together, or owing a purse together." Therefore, the word "fellowship" means to hold something in common.

Fellowship is a word denoting a relationship that is dependent on more than one individual. It is an interdependent, symbiotic, or mutual relationship. As believers gather to fellowship, they contribute to the welfare of each other in the group. We heavily depend on each other for our spiritual, physical, emotional, and psychological needs. Koinoinia is an action word, which is not just being together but taking action together. It is action to pray together, action to teach the word of God, action to encourage one another, action to clothe or shelter one another, action to comfort and console one another in times of difficulties or crises. It is an action of goodwill; a godly centered fellowship is koinoinia.

*"They devoted themselves to the apostles' teaching and to the **fellowship**, to the breaking of bread and to prayer. All the believers were together and had everything in common" (Acts 2:42-44).* The Bible teaches that they devoted themselves to the **didache** (apostles' teaching) and to brotherly fellowship. They took care of each other needs. Anytime you pray together with other believers, you must be aware that koinoinia is taking place in your life.

It demonstrated the binding of people together by the spirit or grouping people in harmony of spirit. It was a voluntary sharing of goods among the members of the community. In the Dead Sea scroll, it is known as *Yahoo* as it describes "the oneness", or "unity". The Jewish community described in the Dead Sea Scroll shared their goods among themselves since they fervently believed in the eminent return of the Savior.

Paul in his apostolic ministry collected offering for the impoverished Christians of the Jerusalem society. This is clearly indicated in Romans 15:26 *"For Macedonia and Achaia were pleased to make a contribution for the poor among the saints in Jerusalem.* The Church in Jerusalem was confronted with social welfare issues. The major problem confronting the Church was the vulnerability of widows. Women and their husbands migrated to Jerusalem in their twilight years to enjoy the beauty of the city. Consequently, their husbands died sooner than later leaving them impoverished. Therefore, the Church had to embark on Charity projects in order to meet the challenges of the first century.

Hence, Romans 15:26 illustrates how the spirit of koinoinia prevailed in the gentile world and among Christians as Paul preached the gospel across kingdoms and territories. In Galations, the apostle stipulates, *"All they asked was that we should continue to remember the poor, the very thing I was eager to do (Gal 2:10).* Paul knew the importance of charity work and the spirit of help, bonding, and friendship even among the impoverished Christians community in Jerusalem. He had hitherto taken care of the poor in the Jerusalem Church and believed that it was imperative for him to exhibit the same godly gesture to them. Paul being an example to many Christians also elaborated on the spirit of koinoinia when he was writing to the Corinthian Church. They were also to contribute to the welfare of Jerusalem Christian community.

*Now about the collection for God's people: Do what I told the Galatian Churches to do. On the first day of every week, each one of you should set in keeping with his income, saving it up, so that when I come no collections will have to be made.....to the men I approved and send them with your gift to Jerusalem."* A majority of people living in Jerusalem was Jews and yet the gentile Churches scattered abroad were willing to contribute enormously to the welfare and upkeep of the Christians in Jerusalem. Jerusalem Christians were living in abject poverty. It was a tangible proof for Paul, Jews, and the gentiles that the spirit of koinoinia bound Christians of different races, tribes, and ethnic affiliations together. It was an empirical evidence of unity, common faith, and common salvation that was the benchmark of their community. Having exhibited outstanding leadership skills and fostering harmony, brotherly love and the spirit of Koinoinia in the Jerusalem Church, the chief apostles, Peter, John and the brother of Jesus, James extended Koinoinia to Paul and Barnabas in Jerusalem in AD 49.

Praying for each other was an empirical evidence of koinoinia. It is imperative that prayer is the life-wire that energizes people to develop unquenchable love and desire for Christ. In addition, because prayer congregates people, it surely magnetizes people of the same faith together. If there seems to be disunity in your Church, cooperate prayer would draw people together forming a formidable unit of believers leading to sound evangelism and progress of the Kingdom of God. Do you want to success? Prayer is the **key** for realization of goals and purposes.

## PRAYER AGAINST CONSPIRACY

When demons, principalities, powers, and diabolical Homo sapiens conspire against you, you must provoke divine assistance through prayer. Jeremiah's prophetic message evoked hostilities against him. Thus, Jeremiah 18:18 is an epitome of how pervasive and massive the opposition is *"They said, come let's make plans against Jeremiah."* They made a plot and devised a plan against him. His prophetic message was not irrationalism, emotionalism or lack of spiritual maturity but God's word spoken to them by a heavily anointed prophet. His message provoked a formidable and intentional opposition to silence him. Like Jesus who had stiff opposition from the priests, elders, and the scribes, Jeremiah's opponents were recalcitrant priests of the communities, and the societies. They included obstinate and sinful people like the "wise", and the false prophets. These represent the power structure of most communities.

They wanted to attack him with their tongue. *"Come let's attack him with our tongue and pay no attention to anything he says."* It was not a gossip or a slander. It was not just a squabble or a short quarrel; it was to summon him before the court of law with the intention of making him a public enemy. If he became a public enemy then, they could have the opportunity to stone him to death or lynching him in any form. Jeremiah's response to the conspiracy is clearly spelt out in the following verses:

> *"Listen to me o, Lord. Hear what my accusers are saying. Give them over to famine, hand them over to the power of the sword let them be made childless and widows. Men be put to death, young men be slain by the sword, and a cry be heard in their houses. Do not forgive their crimes or blot out their sins from their sight. Let them be overthrown by the sword. Deal with them in the time of your anger" (Jer. 18:19-23).*

Similarly, David appeals to the heavenly king, the omnipresent, omniscient, omnipotent God as Jehovah Shabuoth –the divine warrior and judge to come to his defense? David is maliciously attacked by some strong adversaries, so he prays to God for help and to make a woe of his enemies.

> *"Contend, O Lord, with those who contend with me; fight against those who fight against me. Brandish spear and javelin against those who pursue me. May those who seek my life be disgraced and be put to shame. Be turn back in dismay. . May they*

*be like chaff. May their paths be dark and slippery. May ruin overtake them. May the net they hid entangle them. Do not let them wink the eye and be not silent. Do not be far from me. Arise to my defense. Arise to my defense, contend for me, my God and Lord. Vindicate me in your righteousness. May those who gloat over my distress be put to shame and confusion"(Psalm 35:1-28)*

When you are faced with conspiracy of all forms, pray for deliverance, and against demonic opponents who stand in the way of progress. Pray against those who peddle lies about you. Pray against those who orchestrate and perpetrate acts of violence and intimidation against you. Pray that the Lord would extricate you from the jaws of death and catapult you to the highest peak of glory and reputation. Pray for the osmosis of divine peace to permeate your heart and your total being. Do you want to overcome all manners of conspiracy? Then pray, because prayer is the **key** for success.

## Using the Imprecatory Psalms in Prayer

The term imprecations imply "curses" and suggest that the psalmists who faced imminent danger prayed that evil and misfortune will befall their adversaries or persecutors. Biblical scholars view it as a strong term and perhaps not the most accurate one to use. They believe terms such as "psalms of anger", or "Psalms of wrath" should be used instead. Scholars have identified seven psalms, which fall into this category. These are psalms 35, 55, 59, 69, 79, 109, and 137. Of these psalms 35, 69, and 109 are the fiercest, even though the others have some level of venom to frustrate the efforts of persecutors and adversaries. Metaphorically, their enemies were pictured as "lions" (35:17), or "snarling dogs who prowl about the city (59:6, 14-15). Their ravenous temperament is highly manifested in the phrase, "blood thirsty men" (59:2). The psalmist recognized that those who orchestrated and perpetrated evil against him were his friends. He also observed that his accusers had no reason for perpetrating evil and malicious deeds against him. He declares, "For wicked and deceitful men have opened their mouths against me." (Psalm109: 2-3). In view of this, the psalmist recognized he was suffering for the Lord's sake. Even though men and women had forsaken him, he had dauntless faith in God. He also discerned that the community had favor before him and he had a sense of belonging. Some hoped for his vindication (35:27). In conclusion, curses were meant to pronounce judgment upon his enemies.

For instance, the first King of Israel after forsaking the decrees and commands of God, Yahweh made him the fiercest adversary of King David. On several occasions, he sought for the life of David. He sent emissaries to lynch David in his house, and threw a javelin against him when David sat playing the harp for him. He took swift action to destroy David, when he was informed of his location (1 Sam 23:7-8, 19-23; 24:1-2; 26:1-2). He also cast a javelin at Jonathan, when he tried to marshal support for David (20:32-33). Saul also decimated the entire city of NOB when he found out that the priests of the city had shown benevolent attitude towards David loyalists (21: 1-9; 22:7-19).

Under such a life threatening circumstance, David had the right to pray against his enemies. In all these traumatizing situations, David escaped death partly because of his prayer nature, and partly because he was a righteous man in the eyes of God and his fellow Israelites. Imprecatory prayer will extricate you from the entangled web of assassins, and executioners. Imprecatory prayer is sharper than a doubled edge sword, which is competent of pulling down strongholds, tearing down demonic foundations, and planting the seed of goodness in your life. Imprecatory prayer is as potent as a biological or chemical warhead, capable of decimating satanic kingdoms and territories, and any principality that serves as an impediment to your advancement. Imprecatory prayer will make you a winner in every battle and not a loser. It will make you a champion in every life endeavor and not a mediocre.

## PRAYER COMFORTS

Prayer comforts you in times of crisis. Comfort results from trauma, sicknesses, misfortunes, calamities, disasters and miserable circumstances that befall humanity. The word comfort is so important when it comes to Church administration, in medicine, business organizations, communities, families, and in our societies. Usually, during time of crises or a natural disaster, we expect to receive comfort from our loved ones and people who are at the helm of affairs of our lives. Therefore, our God is a comforter. Cry to him and he will comfort you. He will uphold you with his righteous hand and will bestow his divine providence and peace upon you. You are never alone when you cry to him in prayer. The Hebrew word for comfort is **nacham** meaning *to be consoled, to have compassion, to comfort oneself, to suffer grief, and to be relieved.* In Jeremiah 30:11, God declares that he is the comforter. "You *have turned my mourning into dancing; you have taken off my sackcloth and clothed me with joy.*"

After God punished Jerusalem and Israel by taking them to exile, he promised to comfort them. Beware that certain problems such as financial malfeasance, embezzlement and misappropriation might have caused you so much pain, embarrassment and shame. Certain acts of sexual promiscuity might have plunged you into the abyss of shame and spiritual bankruptcy. Beware that certain bad habits such as drug addiction, fighting and riot lifestyle might have brought great toll of suffering and depravity to you. Nevertheless, in all these difficulties and woes, God wants you to know that he is the comforter. Victims of 9/11/2001 needed our comfort (nacham). Victims of cardiovascular diseases, and gastric bypass need the comfort of Christians.

God is making a clarion call to you, indicating that he is ready to comfort you. In Jeremiah 31:15-17 God's word to mother Rachel is an invitation to wipe away her tears, to end the weeping. "For the children who are not will be." The gift of hope overrides the despair of the lamenter. Comfort is given when you call on God. You might have lost your house through flood or through fire, be comforted and call on God for help. You might have also lost a house due to the current socio-economic difficulties belching out of the credit crunch; the lord sends you a word of comfort. For what seemed to have been totally lost will be recovered and your glory be given to you. Only call on God. Even when you go through dangers, calamities, and perilous circumstances, the Lord says he would comfort you.

*"Even though I walk through the valley of the shadow of death, I will fear no evil, for you are with me; your rod and your staff, they* comfort me. *(Ps 23:4).* The rod of the Lord will console you. Every good shepherd **comforts (nacham)** the wounded sheep. He treats them, cares for them and reinvigorates them. Our God will comfort you and console you in times of disaster.

The shepherd's rod is used to guard and guide the sheep. It is also used to rescue and protect the sheep from ferocious wolves and other ravenous animals. Therefore, in this verse, God is informing you to be aware that, he will protect you. He whispers to you to be aware that he will rescue you from every trouble and difficulty. At times, the rod of the shepherd is used to scold the sheep. Therefore, when you stray from the path of righteousness, he disciplines you but bestows his manifold blessings upon you. The staff of the Lord is also used to support the shepherd and uphold him in all circumstances. You will be supported by the Lord and be upheld in every difficult situation. The verse also expounds on the road between Jerusalem and Jericho. It was a dangerous road to travel. It was a haven for career criminals who waylaid travelers and robbed them of their possessions. In some instances, some were maimed for life or killed. The parable of the Good Samaritan illustrated in Luke 10: 25-37 constitutes an archetype of walking through the valley of the shadow of death. It is in view of this that David, the writer of the psalm, says he will fear no evil because God is with him. Know that God is perpetually with you and will always save you from ferocious animals, and ravenous wolves of your life.

Psalm 86:17 indicates, *"give me a sign of your goodness, that my enemies may see it and be put to shame, for you, O, Lord, have helped me and comforted me."* The Lord would not only comfort you, he would also increase your honor, integrity and reputation in your community and your family. He would also make his goodness, which is enshrined in you to be made explicit to everyone. Even those who wished you were plunged into desperation and destruction would see your goodness shine forth like the rising morning star. Why? Because the Lord is your helper and comforter. If you desire to overcome 21$^{st}$ century calamitous activities orchestrated and perpetrated against you, then pray. The reason is that prayer is the **key** for success, growth and prosperity.

## SHEPHERD (PSALM 23: 1-5)

Comprehending the theological and Biblical implication of the 23$^{rd}$ Psalm will help provide spiritual as well physical panacea to famished souls and the emotionally troubled. It may even act as hope and confidence to the fatherless. Biblical scholars have unanimously concurred that the most appraised psalm used to illustrate the guiding nature of God is Psalm 23. The Psalm begins with a metaphor. The employment of a metaphor unravels all that it connotes in regular verbal and written communication to the analysis of the subject matter to which it is intricately related. "A metaphor conveys more, and it speaks more powerfully than it is possible to do in a discursive speech. It draws on various experiences that evoke imagination of the reader. It is therefore decorative in connotation, capable of polysemy."[1] Thus, the commencement metaphorical expression is an indication that the entire psalm is composed in a metaphorical idiom. That has firmly established the psalm as a poem exhibiting a powerful poetic endurance as a psalm of faith. The psalm therefore makes an intensive use of the term "shepherd" which becomes the nerve center of the psalm, and controls the entirety of it[2].

---

[1] James Luther Mays, *Psalms, Interpretation: A Biblical Commentary for Teaching and Preaching* (Louisville Kentucky: John Knox Press, 1994), 116.
[2] Ibid., 116.

The term "shepherd" was rich, and complex notion in the Israelite culture as the relationship of the shepherd to his flock was well accustomed in peasant communities. The cardinal occupations of the shepherd's were to protect, and provide for the flock. The shepherd pastured the flock, led them through stream ways, and right ways, and fended off predators. The sheep were his core responsibility and he accounted for their welfare and safety. Using "shepherd" as imagery, the notion transcends beyond activities of animal husbandry to embrace divine love, and protection for his people. The word makes a clarion call to the clergy to emulate the true meaning of divine care in order to shine out the glory of God to their members.[3] In the Ancient near East therefore, the role and title of shepherd was designated to leaders as they discharged their responsibilities to the people. As a vocative, "shepherd" came to connote royalty. God and kings of Israel were designated the title, "shepherds" of the people. As a result, in the kingdom, God is our shepherd, caring, providing, and protecting us always. God and kings are described with specific nouns (mace), the rod and the shepherd's staff as authority of office. The shepherd's rod is also used to guard and guide the sheep. It is also used to rescue and protect the sheep from ferocious wolves, lions, bears, and other ravenous animals. In the Pentateuch, the psalms and in the prophets, the LORD is called the shepherd of Israel, and his flock in (Gen. 49:9; Ps. 28: 9; 74:1; 95:7; 100:3; Jer. 31:10; Micah 7:14). The Lord made David his special shepherd (Ps.78: 70-72), and the kings of Israel were judged as shepherd and not as common people (Jer. 23:1-4; 49:20; Micah 5:4). Furthermore, the title has special meaning with the Lord's leading and protecting his people in the wilderness (Pss. 77:20; 78:52-53; 80:10) and return from exile (Isa.40:11; 49:9-10).[4]

Mays further illustrates "The Lord is my shepherd" portrays all richness of theological, biblical, social and political background as well as the pastoral domain of the shepherd. The expression is an epitome of trust and commitment to God. It is a zenith of polemical

[3] Ibid., 116.
[4] Ibid.,117.

12

trust as against human rulers and divine powers. The psalms entrusts life complexities, guidance, providence, and protection only to the one whose name is *Yahweh.*[5] The expression, "I shall not be in want" in Psalm 23:1 is worthy of explication. For instance, during forty years wandering in the scorching and perilous desert, the Israelites lacked nothing (Deut. 2:7). David specifically declares in Psalm 34: 10, "The lion may grow weak and hungry, but those who seek the LORD, lack no good things." Since the Lord is a good "shepherd, the psalmist declares, "He restores my soul" in verse three, which is a declaration of trust and total dependence on God. The restoration of life is significant for the survival, peace and tranquility of the individual, and the community as they offer thanksgiving to God (Pss. 30:3; 116:7; 80:3, 7; 44:25; Lam. 1:11, 16-19). "He leads me in the path of righteousness" resonates with Pss. 5:8; 27: 11; 77:20). Correspondingly, Exodus 15:13 depicts, the Lord leading the people like a flock to the holy pastures.[6] The psalmist declares, "For you are with me" in verse four, is an archetype of salvation addressed to those who are in danger of perishing. For example, the road between Jerusalem and Jericho was dangerous to travel on. It was a haven for career criminals who waylaid travelers and robbed them of their possessions. In some instances, some were maimed for life or killed. The parable of the Good Samaritan illustrated in Luke 10: 25-37 constitutes a prototype example of walking through the valley of the shadow of death. It is in view of this that David, the writer of the psalm, says he will fear no evil because God is with him. The lord always declares to his people, "fear not, I am with you" (Gen 15:1; 26:24; Deut. 20:1; 31:8; Isa. 41:10, 13; 43:5). Additionally, "you prepare a table before me" is an imagery describing a feast, which was part of rituals of thanksgiving. In other words, in the Ancient near east covenants were often concluded with a meal expressive of their bond

---

[5] Ibid., 117.

[6] James Luther Mays, *Psalms, Interpretation: A Biblical Commentary for Teaching and Preaching* [Louisville Kentucky: John Knox Press, 1994], 118. See Craigie, Peter C. Psalms1-50, *World Biblical Commentary, Vol. 19.*(Waco, Tex: Word Books, 1983), 207

of friendship (Pss. 22:22-26; 116:13). *Yahweh* prepared a table before Israel in the wilderness (Ps. 78:19).[7] The psalmist demonstrates that "Goodness", the benefit of blessing, and *hesed* (loving kindness), which is the basis for unfathomable deliverance shall pursue him all the days of his life. Thus, dwelling in the house of God continually is an imagery of constant protection from the enemies who likewise pursue the worshipper.[8]

In the New Testament the expression, "The Lord is my shepherd" is designated to Jesus Christ. In John 10:11, Jesus declares, "I am the good shepherd." The disciples of Jesus saw him to be their shepherd and guardian in the kingdom of God (1 Peter 2:25; 5:4). Edmond Clowney, states, "Jesus is not only the good shepherd who gives his life for the sheep; he is also the seeking shepherd, the Lord who gathers his remnant flocks."[9] The chief shepherd, Christ will appear at the consummation and will bestow a crown of glory on all believers that will never be removed (1Peter 5:4). Therefore, the coming of the great shepherd of the sheep (believers) must remind all pastors and the clergy of their daunting responsibility of caring for the flock. At his impending arrival, believers will possess their birthright that is theirs in Christ. They will receive a crown that will sparkle with divine glory. The Greek word translated *crown* describes any circlet, whether of gold, silver, laurel or flowers, and the expression, "that will never fade away" is translated as *amarantinos* signifying unsurpassable glory, beauty and honor. It is a symbol of perpetuity, and immortality.[10] Mays in concluding his discussion on psalm 23

---

[7] Ibid., 118.

[8] Ibid., 118.

[9] Edmond Clowney, *The Messege of 1 Peter* (Downers Grove, Illinois: Intervarsity Press, 1988), 123. The imagery of a seeking shepherd illustrated in John 10:10:16, and Luke 15:5-7is attested in the Old Testament promise in Ezekial 34 where God condemns and judges the false shepherd for not seeking the lost (34: 6, 8) and promises to seek and gather his scattered sheep (34:11-13). The verb is used in active mood to describe turning to the Lord in Acts 11:21; I Thess.1:9.

[10] Ibid., 207.

perspicaciously declares, "Jesus as the shepherd in David's place, is the one who restores our souls, leads us in the path of righteousness, accompanies us through danger, spreads the holy supper before us in the presence of sin and death, and pursues us in gracious love all the days of our lives."[11]

## GOD PREPARES A TABLE BEFORE YOU IN THE PRESENCE OF YOUR ENEMIES WHEN YOU PRAY

Psalm 23: 5 is an archetype of how God provides for you in times of danger and to the astonishment of your adversaries. The Psalmist declares, "You prepare a table before me in the presence of my enemies" In the Ancient near east, covenants were often concluded with a meal expressive of their bond of friendship. God made a covenant with Abraham, which is known as Abrahamic covenant. In this covenant, God promised to bless the descendants of Abraham. Scripture states, *"I will make you into a great nation and I will bless you, I will make your name great, and you will be a blessing. I will bless those who bless you, and whoever curses you, I will curse; and all peoples on earthwill be blessed through you" (Gen 12:2-3)*

This passage dilates on the call of Abraham and the blessing that he was to receive from God. God specifically requested him to leave the land of his fathers in order to journey to a different land where he was to receive unfathomable blessing from the Lord. His call and covenant with God came with untold blessings. Abraham was to be made into a great nation. In other words, the descendants of Abraham would multiply and fill the surface of the earth. Numerically, they were to be uncountable, in strength, they were to be fortified and invincible. There is ample evidence in the Bible that Abraham is the father of the Hebrew people (Genesis 12-23). According to the Old Testament, the history of the Israelites began when God called Abraham and sent him from Mesopotamia to the Land of Canaan to

---

[11] James Luther Mays, *Psalms, Interpretation: A Biblical Commentary for Teaching and Preaching* (Louisville Kentucky: John Knox Press, 1994), 119.

become the ancestral father of God's people. Abraham was to salvage humankind from condemnation to hell because of the fall of Adam and Eve by spreading the message of redemption to the entire world. Consequently, Abraham became the *father of the Hebrew people.* The Bible declares,

Another aspect of his call was to make his name great. His life was going to be characterized with fame on earth. In other words, his name was to be known throughout the world as a great personality, the friend of God and a patriarch who was chosen to bless all nations. Abraham was also going to be a blessing. He was to be prosperous, great and mighty among his peers. Sicknesses and diseases were not part of his physiological make up. His metabolism was devoid of infectious diseases. He did not have to suffer from any cardiovascular disease. God blessed his entire life. When God prepares a table before you in the presence of your enemies, he is assuring you of the Abraham's covenant blessings. That is you would be fabulously rich. You would be showered with good health and have fame and glory in your entire life.

Since blessings were part of the Jewish society, the associates of Abraham, friends and people living in his community and in the foreign land he was to journey to were to bless him. In addition, those who were wise to bless Abraham, God would exude his manifold blessings upon them. And since curses were also part of the society at that time, and still pervade in the 21st century, God promised Abraham that he was combat-ready to curse those who cursed him.

Genesis 17:1-5 *"is the focal point of the Abrahamic materials. It is the center piece in which all the important aspects of Abraham's life come together."* God changed his name from Abram to Abraham at the age of ninety-nine. He changed Sarah's name from Sarai to Sarah. He was now to be a *"Father of many nations"*. A change in name signifies a new reality, a changed status before God. God changed Saul to Paul, Simon to Peter, and Jacob to Israel. Sarah at this point was assured that despite her senile age of 89, she was going to conceive and give birth to a baby boy of destiny within a year. A covenant changes your destiny to prosperity and glory. A divine covenant changes every barren project in your life and turning it into a productive 21st Century business venture. Even though it took Sarah and Abraham 25 years to have their long awaited son, their destiny was changed when Isaac was born. Every covenant signed with God brings changes in your life. In the Patriachal and Jewish society, childlessness was scorned upon. Nevertheless, the covenant with God erased every form of contempt, scorn, embarrassment, and disgrace in their lives.

In this chapter, God signed a covenant (**berit**) with Abraham. The term **berit** occurs thirteen times in 22 verses (17:1-22). It is abundantly clear that God had established a unique, permanent, and binding relationship with Abraham. Having indicated this, Abraham who is an epitome of biblical character with unflinching faith in God illustrates Christian Doctrine of conversion. Fortunately, the promise that God made to Abraham was fulfilled. Isaac was born when Sarah was 90 years old while Abraham was 100 years of age. Then in verse 8, God states, *"The whole land of Canaan, where you are now an alien, I will give as an everlasting possession to you and your descendants after you, and I will be their God."*

God will give you the ability and wisdom to possess whatever he promises in his word and covenant. You are to possess the materials blessings of Abrahamic covenant. You are to possess the spiritual blessings of the Abrahamic covenant. You are deemed to possess family blessings of the Abrahamic covenant. You are poised to take hold of community blessings of the Abrahamic covenant. You are well equipped to possess the gold and silver of the nations because you are part of the Abrahamic covenant. When God prepares a table before you in the presence of your enemies, you would succeed where they thought you would fail. You would emerge victoriously in every spiritual combat to possess your territory.

# God Anoints You for Greater Works When You Pray

The official name, Christ has its Old Testament equivalent, **Meshiach,** from Mashach, **"to anoint",** and hence means "the anointed one." It was customarily for priests, kings, and leaders in the Old Testament to be anointed for honorable tasks, Ex. 29:7; Lev. 4:3; judegs 9:8; 1 Sam 9:16; 10:1; 2 Sam 19:10. The king or the designated leader was called " the anointed of Yahweh", 1 Sam 24:10. The anointing of a prophet is also recorded once in 1 Kings 19:16. There are references to prophetic anointing in Psalm 105:15, Isaiah 61: 1[12]

The oil used in anointing the Yahweh leaders symbolized the *spirit of God (Ruah),* Isaiah 61:1; zech 4:1-6. The anointing symbolized the transfusing or transfer of the spirit of God to the consecrated person, 1 Sam 10:1-6; 16:13-14. The anointing was a visible sign of (1) an **appointment to office, (2)** the establishment of a sacred relationship and the consequent of sacrosanctness of the person anointed, 1 Sam 24:6; 26:9; 2 Sam 1:14. (C) This is divine transfer of the Spirit to the anointed one, 1 Sam 16:13; 2Cor 1:21-22. Furthermore, the Old Testament authenticates the overpowering of anointing of the Lord in Psalm 2:2; 45:7, and the New Testament asserts that anointing of the Lord in Acts 4:27; and 10:38.[13]

Another word used in the Old Testament to refer to anointing of the Lord is *nasak.* It is used in Psalm 2:6; prov. 8:23. The connotation associated with this word is " to set up" rather than "to anoint." Thus, it appropriate to emphasize that Christ was set up or appointed from eternity to become the savior of humankind.[14]

It is imperative to authenticate that historically, his anointed commenced with the conception. He was conceived by the Holy

---

[12] Luis Berkhof, *Systematic Theology* (Grand Rapids, Michigan: William B. Eerdmans, 1996), 312
[13] Ibid, 312
[14] Ibid; 312

Spirit, Lk 1:35, and was overpowered and energized by the holy Spirit at his baptism.[15]

The baptism of Jesus in Mark 1:9-11, and the transfiguration of Jesus Christ in Mark 9:2-8 were events that brought about a magnificent infilling and out pouring of the Holy Spirit on him. At the baptism, he received an immeasurable amount of the Holy Spirit making him valiant and invincible in his ministry as he proclaimed the kingdom of God. The baptism of Jesus in the synoptic gospels is followed immediately by the temptation in the wilderness. However, Jesus like Paul became fully aware that God called him on the occasion of divine vision. Justin Martyr and the gospel of Ebionites subscribe God's utterances to Jesus at his baptism with the enthronement of King David in Psalm 2:7 *"this day I have begotten thee."* The term *agapetos* denoting *"beloved"* also conveys the semantic representation of *"doomed to death"* since the term is literally translated in the Hebrew Bible, *yahid*, meaning "only child", "uniqueness", solidarity". It is actually used in a context of an only child who is either in recent times died or just about to die, (cf. used of only son and only daughter, Gen 22:2,12,16; Jer. 6:26; Judges 11.34).[16]

The term "messiah" is the translation of the Hebrew term *masiah*, which is derived from the verb *masah*, meaning to smear or anoint. When objects such as wafers and shields were smeared with grease or oil they were said to be anointed; hence the commonly used term was "anoint" when grease or oil was applied to objects by Israelites and non-Israelites

Thus, anointing is so paramount in the ministry of a pastor or the believer. PSALM 23: 5b states, **"You anoint my head with oil my cup overflows."** If shepherds are to make an impact on their ministry, they must consciFentiously seek the **anointing**.

In Exodus 30: 26, a type of oil was prepared and its main purpose was to be used in anointing the different parts of the Tabernacle,

---

[15] Ibid; 313

[16] Eduard Schweizer, *The Good News According to Matthew* (Atlanta, Georgia: John Knox Press, 1975),339

including the priests. The principal reason for anointing them was to set the individuals and special objects apart, and to sanctify them. Exodus 30: 30 *"Anoint Aaron and his sons and consecrate them so they may serve me as priests."* The anointing was meant to set Aaron and his descendants apart for the priestly office where they administered before God. They were enjoined to be sanctified so that in coming to God they could be holy and would be able to perform the duties that God had entrusted to them. Anointing is to set you apart so that you will be fortified by supernatural force to carry out godly assignments. Anyone, who ever performed miracles in the Bible did not achieve it by carnality or by satanic whimsical manipulations. He received it directly from the Living God. Scripture declares, *"Then Samuel took a flask of oil, poured it on Saul's head, and kissed him, saying, "Has not the Lord anointed you leader over his inheritance?(1Sam.10:1).*Samuel said to Saul that he was going to meet a company of prophets and he would be changed into another man and would prophesy with them. 1 Samuel 10:6 *"The spirit of the Lord will come upon you in power, and you will prophesy with them; and you will be changed into a different person."*

> *1Samuel 10:9 "As Saul turned to leave Samuel, God changed Saul's heart, and these signs were fulfilled."*

When you receive the anointing of God, you would perform kingly duties. You would have a divine purpose to accomplish on earth. If you lack vision and direction in life, the anointing demonstrates to you what you are to achieve in life. The anointing would make you a winner, and not a loser. Where others fail, you would succeed because of the anointing. After Saul received the anointing, he stopped running helter-skelter after his father's animals and prophesied with the prophets. He assumed a kingly position. The anointing would establish you and give you a sense of purpose. If you did not know what to do to be an achiever, the anointing would draw up the road map to success for you.

## ANOINTING THE SICK IN PRAYER (JAMES 5:13-18)

James, the writer of the epistle has spilt much ink on the subject of praying and anointing the sick. From chapter 5: 13-18, prayer is mentioned in every verse. Prayer is introduced in verse 13 as a response to suffering and praising God in songs as a response of feeling joyful and happy in life. In those days, healing of the sick through anointing by a priest was evaluated as a sacrament. This provoked the debate between the Catholic Church and the reformers concerning the number of sacraments available in the church. At the council of Trend session 14 (DBS 1716-19), they stressed that extreme auction was a sacrament instituted by Christ and reinforced by James. Elders were not just mere community members, but priests ordained by the Bishop.

In praying for the sick, the elders, including the apostles had miraculous gifts of healing. This is indicated in (Acts 3: 6; 5:15; 14:8-10; 28 :). In AD 50s, in the Church of Corinth, a number of disciples were recognized as having the charism of the gift of healing (1 Cor12: 9, 28, 30). In the Gospels, anointing is also viewed as medicinal as indicated in Luke 10:34, in the case of the good Samaritan or an accompaniment to prayer for the sick as clearly demonstrated in Matthew 6: 13. Throughout James, there are echoes of Jesus' tradition and hence the practice prescribed in James 5: 13-18 might have been implied that Jesus commanded it.

The tool used in anointing the sick was Olive oil. This was used as a source of medicine in the former times. In Lev 14: 10-32, anointing with oil is a sign of one having been cleansed from leprosy. The Prophet Isaiah indicates that wounds are healed or softened by oil while Jeremiah suggests the healing power of the balm of Gilead. Prayer accompanied with anointing does not only heal the person, but cleanses the spirit, soul and mind of the healed. It extricates them from spiritual and psychological trauma and improves their self -image. Anointing the sick via prayer has proven to work miracles in the Pentecostal and charismatic denominations over the years. Victims of demon-possessed personalities are known to have been set free from the shackles of bondage. Over the years, I have used the anointing oil to anoint and perform miracles in the lives of people. In 1995, a young man felt sick because of mental incapacitation. This glorious man had abandoned his university studies, and travelled home. On arrival, he vandalized his home electronics and gadgets due to hysteria associated with his predicament. After failing to find a cure to the disease, my elder brother directed him to me for Christocentric prayers. After I prayed a couples of times with him, and anointing him with oil he was restored to good health, and went back to the university to complete his program. He is now a High School teacher in Tamale, Ghana. Anointing coupled with faith will heal the sick.

Homogeneously, over the years, sicknesses are known to have been cured via praying and anointing the sick with olive oil through me in the name of Jesus in Church, on parks, and in apartments. In Tamale, Ghana, demons were exorcised from several people as a result of Christomorphic and Christocentric prayers. Children were delivered from premature deaths, students of mine set free from demonic harassment, Church members delivered from emotional and demonic captivity. Prayer accompanied with faith and anointing has supernatural potency to heal the sick, and to liberate the demon-possessed from torment

Prayer of faith offered by the elder would restore the sick person was a continuation from the Old Testament. Psalm 35: 13-14 is a classic example of visiting friends and praying for them. For instance, Job friends who visited him wanted to pray for him so that if he had sinned, his sin could be forgiven. A connection between sickness and sin is also illustrated in 1Cor 11: 29-30, where many are sick, weak, and dying. Elijah was a man of faith who prayed for the cessation of rain for 3 ½ years and God answered his prayers. He did pray again and the windows of heaven burst open and poured out torrential rains.

## KNOW THAT JESUS IS THE ALPHA AND THE OMEGA OF YOUR LIFE WHEN YOU PRAY

The alpha and Omega are the first and the last letters of the Greek alphabets. When Jesus says He is the alpha and the Omega, it means He is the total representation or revelation of God. He is overall. The term *Alpha and Omega* comes from the phrase "I am the alpha and the omega" (Koiné Greek: "ἐγὼ τὸ Α καὶ τὸ Ω"), an appellation of Jesus[17] in the Book of Revelation (verses 1:8, 21:6, and 22:13). The first part of this phrase ("I am the Alpha and Omega") is first found in Chapter 1 verse 8, and is found in every manuscript of Revelation that has 1v8. Several later manuscripts repeat "I am the Alpha and Omega" in 1v11 too, but it does not receive support here from most of the oldest manuscripts, including the Alexandrine, Sinaitic, and **Codex Ephraemi Rescriptus**. Nevertheless, it is omitted in some post-modern translations. Scholar Robert Young states, with regard to "I am the Alpha and Omega" in 1v11, that the "oldest [manuscripts] omit" it.[18] In fact, he is the embodiment of God. It is the expressing of Christ nature that Christ Himself gave, "I am the alpha and the Omega, the beginning and the end." The Book of revelation begins with two (Rev. 1:8, 11) references to this title, and ends with two of the same (Rev. 21:6; 22:13). These verses mean that Jesus essence embraces eternity of all times, He is the Lord of the church and every household. Revelation 21: 6-7 and 22: 12-13 educate that Christ is always by our side wiping away our tears, making all things new, drawing water from the fountain of life to anyone who is thirsty. He is the comforter, the one who prospers us. The prophet Isaiah echoes a similar sentiment in **43:18-19 "Forget the former things; do not dwell on the past. See, I am doing a new thing! Now it springs up; do you not perceive it? I am making a way in the desert and streams in the wasteland."** When you pray,

---

[17] CCL.ORG (Accessed on July 2, 2014), 1

[18] *Young's Concise Commentary on the Holy Bible*, Robert Young, p. 180, 1977

know that God through Jesus is doing a new thing in your life. He wipes away your tears and replaces mourning with joy. Prayer in the name of Jesus will enable you to subdue your past mistakes knowing that Jesus is doing a new thing in your life. What appears to be unproductive in your life will produce in a hundred fold. You will subdue what seems insurmountable in the natural eye. Prayer has the ability to erase the venom of your past mistakes and diabolical deeds leading you to become a fervent productive agent of God. Prayer will illuminate your natural eyes and heart, making heaven to bestow upon you prosperity of his kingdom. Where there seems to be lack of productivity, prayer will make you a productive agent of God. Where there appears to be lack of progress, prayer will energize you with progressive ideas. If you were failing or have failed, know that prayer will reinstate you and make you the most valiant and prosperous personality of your time. Do you really want to be different and succeed in this 21ˢᵗ century economic struggles, earthquakes, fires, loss of jobs, plane crashes, train derailments, tsunamis, hurricanes, tornados, plagues, accidents, shootings, and calamities, then pray. Is your, **once prospered** businesses liquidated or is about to be liquidated? Then use prayer to overcome all of them. Ladies and Gentlemen, fellow believers in the vineyard of the Lord, prayer is the **key** for accomplishment, protection and enjoyment of life.

## KNOW THAT YOU ARE MORE THAN A CONQUEROR

A reason why so many people are defeated in life is that they do not know who they are in the Lord. The Bible teaches in Roman 8: 37 that in all these things we are more than conquerors. Know that in trouble or in hardship, you are more than a conqueror. Beware that in famine or nakedness you are more than a conqueror. Speak words of a conqueror and not words of a defeated warrior. The koine Greek term for *more than a conqueror is* **hupermikao or hupermike.** The word connotes, *victor, a winner, an overcomer, a vanquisher, subjugator, captor, to annex.* Speak words of a champion not words of the conquered. Speak words of a winner and not words of a loser. If you know this, you will emerge as a winner in every battle. If you know this, you will always be a DAVID and therefore you will overpower every GOLIATH in your life. In 2Co.2: 14, Paul says, *Now thanks be unto God, which always causeth us to triumph in Christ, and maketh manifest the savour of his knowledge by us in every place.* We are destined to triumph over every difficulty and circumstance in our lives. You should know that in Christ you could triumph over sicknesses and diseases, poverty, family problems etc. You are not just a conqueror but you are more than a conqueror because he who is in you is greater than the one outside. Christ in you the hope of glory. David was more than a conqueror. Samson wielded the might and authority to subdue the Philistines. You are more than a conqueror when you pray. Mohammad Ali was more than a conqueror in his boxing career. There was no foe, and no opponent that could withstand his deadly punches. His punches were packed with venom that sent his enemies crushing to the floor. He knew who he was; he spoke what he knew and delivered what he said. Invincibility was his portion. Despite all odds, he rose up to be the most versatile, dexterous, invincible boxer whose fighting prowess could not be challenged by any human endeavor since the beginning of creation. He was primus interparis (First among his equals). Just as Deborah, Jehu, David, Samson, Othniel, Solomon, Paul, Peter, and above all Jesus were invincible in their careers; you will be more than a conqueror if you pray. Do you want to succeed in these perilous times? Then pray, because prayer is the **key** for attainment of your goals, dreams and visions.

## BE HUMBLE WHEN YOU PRAY

Humility is an important ingredient in Godly centered prayer. According to the indelible word, God opposes the proud but uplifts and promotes the humble. It is in view of this that humility of the Christian is paramount in every facet of their lives especially when it comes to the life-wire of prayer. The chief apostle being so conversant with this declares, "Young men in the same way be submissive to those who are older. All of you clothe yourself with **humility** toward one another, because "God opposes the proud but gives grace to those who are humble" (1Peter 5:5). The Greek term for **humility** is *khamalos* meaning "on the ground, low, trifling." Another word used to refer to humility is is *tapinos* which has the same meaning as *khamalos*. Actually, humility and meekness are used parallel in the New Testament. The word "meek" has another connotation worthy of explanation. Wherever the Greek word translated "meek" or "humble" (*pra- yes*) occurs in the Bible it always signifies peacefulness or peacemaking. For example, Matthew 21: 5 is a quote from Zechariah 9:9. The God to whom we surrender is "the God of peace" (Rom15: 33). God is a universal lover and a peacemaker. He causes the rain and the sunshine to bestow blessings on our enemies as well as our friends. He admonishes us to love our enemies (Mt 5: 43-48). Martin Luther King Jr said, "Jesus understood the difficulty inherent in the act of loving one's enemy.…. He realized that every genuine expression of love grows out of a consistent and total surrender to God" (King, Strength to love, 48).[19]

Jesus did not only expound on this but emanated God's love and meekness to his disciples, tax collectors, outcasts, and Gentiles. He welcomed all of them into the Kingdom of God for divine fellowship. Archbishop Dmitri Royster affirms, "The meek are those who live, conscious of their own unworthiness, with patience and in peace with their fellow men. Those who live in hostility with others cannot enter the kingdom of God, the new earth which the meek shall inherit."[20] The literal sense of the word "meek" or "gentleness" refers to those who make no claims for themselves before God or other people. The zealots in Jewish community claimed their rights. Thus, in this context, it is those who push, who struggle, who get their piece of land. Admirably, Jesus does not say, "The gentle may inherit

[19] Ibid., 41.
[20] Archbishop Dmitri Royster, *The Kingdom of God* [Crestwood, New York: St. Vladimir's Press, 1992], 26.

heaven," but they will be given the earth. It means that the earth is the sphere of the kingdom of God, this renewed earth."[21]

Jesus quotes from Psalm 37: 11, which declares, "But the meek will inherit the land and enjoy great peace". The Hebrew word used for "meek" has the same connotation with the Greek word employed in Matthew 5:5. The meek in this context deals with people who recognize their spiritual depravity and surrender to God in order to be rescued from sin, trouble, and damnation.[22] If you are economically as well as spiritually poor, and you surrender to God, he is capable of delivering you with his out stretched arm. If you are encumbered with social enigma, surrendering to God will extricate you from social, psychological, and mental gymnastics. In English language however, the word "meek" implies "weak", "harmless", or "spiritless." A meek personality is considered a doormat where others clean off their dirty feet, he is timorous and qualms about what others think.[23] On the contrary, the Biblical language use of this word is in total variance from English implication. The word is used to describe two significant personalities, Moses (Num. 12:3), and Jesus Christ in (Mt 11:29). Moses subdued the seemingly invincible Egyptian might, and a pungent Roman representative could not cow Jesus. Both of them appeared absolutely dauntless, and surrendered their will and emotions to God.[24]

The Hebrew root for *pride is* **gh.** The common term used in the Old Testament is **geon** which occurs numerous times in the rabbinic literature. It actually means cynically insensitive to the needs of others. It denotes conceitedness, arrogance, overweening and haughtiness. The Greek term is **hybris** as indicated in (Acts 27:10, 21; 2 Corinthians 12:10; I Tim 1: 13). The word **hyperephanos** is used in (Mk 7: 22; Lk 1: 51) and four times in the epistles (Rom 1:30;

---

[21]  Ibid., 26.

[22]  Glen H. Stassen & David P. Gushee, *Kingdom of Ethics* (Downers Grove, Illinois: Intervarsity Press, 2003), 40.

[23]  Ibid., 40.

[24]  Ibid., 40.

2 Tim 3:2; James 4:6; I Peter 5:5). Pride of the heart is cancerous, but humility brings favor to you in great dimensions. Pride of the heart blocks and delays your prayers but humility allows your sincere and humble prayer to rise up like incense to the heavens. The principle of humble submission is so clear in this passage. Young men must be in the position to be humble before elders (Church officers).

Peter's clarion call to humility is not limited to the young men only but to all professed and believing Christians. The implication is that the tying on the servant's apron in submission to one another is paramount for enormous spiritual experience. In the verse six of the same chapter, peter states, **"Humble yourselves, therefore, under God's mighty hand, that he may lift you up in due time"** **(1Peter 5:6).** Humility engenders favor, favor stimulates promotion, and promotion leads to success. Advancement in this context depends largely on the extent of your attitude and humility towards God. God expects you to be so humble that you can approach him with important prayer requests. Humility in this context is not a sanctimonious attitude towards God. A sanctimonious attitude is assumption of a false humility towards the supreme commander of the universe. A false humility takes the form of pretending to be holy, when you are so engrossed in sin. False humility seduces you into wallowing in hypocritical lifestyle while accusing others of wrongful behavior. David was a man who exhibited true kind of humility in the Bible. For example, he was remorseful and repentant when he sinned against God by murdering Uriah, and having an amorous relationship with Beersheba. David in humble spirit wrote psalm 51 fervently requesting God to forgive him his sins in the form of clemency, cleansing, restoration, blotting out of transgression, and asking for joy and happiness.

In the same token, James states, "God opposes the proud, but gives grace to the humble." (James 4: 6), and verse 10 declares, "Humble yourselves before the Lord, and he will lift you up." These scriptures dilate on the humility of the worshipper or the individual who calls on the name of the Lord. In humility, you remember the mighty hand of God. God's hand was so mighty to humble the Israelites, purging out the recalcitrant, the rebels, and giving guidance and repentance to his people. Therefore, in these contexts, the chief apostles, Peter and James (brother of the Lord) deal with the mighty hand of God that would uplift the humble from dungeon of life to the glory of life. The mighty hand of God has the ability to make you cross the red sea of your life. The mighty hand of God has the potency to extricate you from financial doldrums to living like a millionaire or a billionaire. The mighty hand of God has the sharpness to lift you from servant hood position to the place of a prince or a king. Even though God humbles, he also uplifts. Vainglorious and acts of pomposity towards God would engender pandemonium, defeat, and failure in your life. On the contrary, a contrite heart would provoke God's mercies on you and he would promote you and would not demote you. You will experience the joy and tranquility of God if you approach him with a humble attitude.

## THOSE WHO WAIT ON THE LORD WILL RENEW THEIR STRENGTH

Waiting on the Lord or hoping in the Lord is one of the greatest characteristics of a prayer warrior or a winner. When you wait on the Lord, you are destined to renew your spiritual fervor and physical energy. Your psychological and mental impetus would be rejuvenated to afford you the opportunity to soar on wings like the eagle. Isaiah 40:31 clearly states, *"But They that wait upon the Lord shall renew their strength; they shall mount up with wings as eagles; they shall run, not be weary; and they shall walk and not faint"* (Is 40:31) KJM.

Eagle Christians wait on the Lord. It is a figure of speech or an imagery illustrating strength and vigor of purpose. It illustrates strength and manly piety, an elevation above the world. A divine communion with the creator and a nearness to his throne. A stage of perfection and sanctification draws the individual or group of worshippers to be so connected to God that they are informed always of his purposes for them and for the world. Even though naturally, an eagle soars into the air and into the sky with little efforts, a child of God who draws his strength from God is given unabated strength to shoot up higher and higher in achieving God-given goals and dreams.

The sentence, *they will run and not grow weary* connotes that those who have unshakable trust in him would be vigorous in their dealing with the Lord. They are the Christians that God depends on for his purposes to be achieved on earth. They are the eagle Christians who refuse to throw in the towel in times of difficulties and calamities. They are the people who are always elevated, unwearied in all that they do. They are dependable, trustworthy, faithful, loyal, holy, pious, and full of heavenly zeal. So that in serving the Lord they will never faint or give up in their calling as Christians.

Eagles can fly up to an altitude of 10,000 feet, but they are able to swiftly land on the ground. Great leaders are **problem solvers**. They don't complain like the crows do. They do not live in roof corners like the sparrows do. Eagles perch on tall trees like the redwood trees and solve hunger problems. Visionary and problem solvers provide for the masses. They are commanders of the air. They are the aeronautical specialists. They are the pilots who never crash planes. They are specialists in the aeronautical industry. They are master pilots who know how to circumvent a threatening cloud or avoid hitting a cyclone or a typhoon. If they happen to hit a cloud, they develop dexterity with the wings, beak and other skills to scale through the cloud or storm. These are the storms we must face as leaders in order to rise up above every challenge. Like an eagle, a leader can only rise to greater heights if he takes up the challenges head on without running away from it. Yet, another leadership characteristics.

Eagles do not fly with crows, and crows do not have the vision of an eagle. A crow cannot fly high into the sky but an eagle can. A chicken does not have the dexterity to fly up to an altitude of 1,000 feet. Eagles love to take challenges as the eagle does when the storm comes. They fly and make less noise waiting for opportunities to strike their next prey or glide with the current of the storm. Eagles are not noise-makers, rather they meditate, and wait silently to pounce on a prey. They know how to take advantage of opportunities. They know when to strike, and the time to wait.

A Christian who relies on God is like the eagle who removes the old feathers, then sprouts up new feathers so that he is able to soar into the sky, coming against strong winds, thunderstorms, hurricanes, cyclones, typhoons, and tornados. As the eagle has the ability to hit against cumulous clouds and penetrate his way up, so is the eagle Christian. He has the spiritual magnetic force to penetrate every obstacle in his or her life. When you wait upon the Lord, you are going to shout up fresh "feathers" that will catapult you into achieving your dreams and goals. Eagles possess great **vitality.** Eagles are full of life and visionary but they find time to look back at their life and re-energize themselves. This happens at about the age of 30. What happens is that when the eagles reach the age of 30, their physical body condition deteriorates fast making it difficult for them to survive.

It is interesting to note that the eagle never gives up leaving. Instead, the eagle retreats to a mountaintop and over a five month period goes through a metamorphosis. It knocks off its own beak by banging it against a rock, plucks out its talons and then feathers. Each stage produces a regrowth of the removed body parts, allowing the eagle to live for another 30 - 40 years.

There are times in your life as a leader that you must look back and take stock of your life. The good and the bad experiences you have been through as a leader. Are you keeping in trend with the current knowledge of ministry? Do you need to improve certain areas in your life as a leader? Are you stuck up with the same old ideas and doing the same thing that wears you out? It is time to behave like the eagle. Remove the old feathers and beak of your life. Your language must be changed and your sermon transformed to meet the needs of the 21st century audience.

In prayer, acknowledge your weakness and humbly request God to strengthen you. When you receive God's strength, you will soar and run like eagles and fight spiritual battles like a champion. When you run with your strength, you will faint, and will utterly fail in your endeavors. However, if you anchor your faith in the Lord, you will be carried above all difficulties. The phrase wait on YAHWEH means to wait for his help. That is to trust him and put your hope in him. It is also applicable to those who are in danger and are seeking deliverance from the almighty God. It is also pertinent to those who are plunged into spiritual bankruptcy, and feel weak, guilty, helpless, shameful, and disgraced.

Eagles have a keen **vision**. Their eyes are specially designed for long distance focus and clarity. They can spot another eagle soaring from 50 miles away as they peach on the tallest trees in the forest. They are able to see a prey far away and swoop upon it, snatching it from its hiding place. Look at great leaders of this world who have come and gone. There are many great leaders that came and went but one characteristic that is common in all is **"Vision"**. Vision is a successful leadership characteristic. While perching on a tree, the body sits still and the head will be tilted side to side to observed what is happening below, around and above it. Even if it's flying close by, you can observe how keen its eyes are looking for its prey. Eagle Christians are great leaders who influence political, social, and economic landscapes of their generations that continue to have positive impact on future generations. Eagles have special binaculors that enables them to spot danger and a prey far from their abode. Eagles Christians are proactive and they know what they look for in life.

Take for Abraham Lincoln for example, the 16th president of the United States, guided his country through the most devastating experience in its national history, the Civil War. He had a vision, to save the union and free the slaves. He is considered by many historians to have been the greatest American president.

Another characteristic of the eagle is that it is **fearless.** An eagle will never surrender to the size or strength of its prey. It will always give a fight to win its prey or regain its territory. Joshua needed the leadership trait of fearlessness when God told him to be strong and courageous. The eagle preys on huge animals larger than its size. It preys on goats, antelopes, bears, and other rapacious animals. Joshua conquered 31 kings before the Israelites possessed the Land. He had to be strong, **FEARLESS** and courageous in order to annihilate the territory of Og, king of Bashan. He reigned in mount Hebron, taking control of the Western Corridor of the River Jordan. He was defeated with the leadership skills of Joshua. Sihon, king of the Amorites was also defeated with the **intelligence of courage.** Thus, Joshua and the Israelites conquered the following kings: **The king of Jericho, the king of Ai (near Bethel), the king of Jerusalem, the king of Hebron, the King of Jarmuth, the king of Lachish, the king of Eglon, the king of Gezer (Joshua 12:1-12).** He conquered the western foothill, the Hittities, the Amorites, Canaanites, Perizzites, Hivites, and Jebusites. He also conquered important cities in the north such as Hazor. In total, Joshua and the people of Yahweh overpowered the land both East (Joshua 12:1-6) and the west (Joshua 12: 7- 27) of the Jordan River. They defeated 31 kings and their cities. With military dexterity coupled with courage and strength **intelligence,** the Israelites vanquished the Hittites, the Amorites, the Canaanites, the Prizzites, the Hivites, and the Jebusites. Joshua defeated enemies and preys larger than the size of Israel.

A person permeated with **courage and strength intelligence** overpowers the financial barriers, work related barriers, political, social, and marital hurdles. With economic meltdown and governments struggling with the **fiscal cliff,** Christians desire the invincibility of the Lord to survive the turbulent times. They need the command of **courage and strength intelligence to eschew mortgage crises, to stem out the venom of unemployment,** to revamp their businesses and to be extricated form poverty, enslavement and contempt. You cannot really possess your **"promised Land"** if you woefully lack **courage and strength intelligence.** Those kings and their people were versatile warriors who knew the military terrain of all territories but with the Lord, the Israelites overcame them. You need the Lord to overpower undesirable kings, undesirable financial embarrassments, nauseating family woes, intellectual and religious belittlement. Successful leaders are fearless. They face problems heard on.[25]

---

[25] http://iandabasorihetr.hubpages.com/hub/7-Leadership-Characteristics-of-An-Eagle-That-Man-Should-Learn-From (Accessed on August 26,2013)

# Eagle Christians are good trainers

Believe this or not. Eagles are known for their aggression. They are absolutely ferocious aren't they? Anyone who doesn't have a total knowledge of this great bird will say yes. What is more astonishing with this bird is their ability to nurture their young ones. Research has shown that no member of the bird family is more gentle and attentive to its young ones than the eagles. This is how it happens. When the mother eagle sees that time has come for it to teach the eaglets to fly, she gathers an eaglet onto her back, and spreading her wings, flies high. Suddenly she swoops out from under the eaglet and allows it to fall. As it falls, it gradually learns what its wings are for until the mother catches it once again. The process is repeated. If the young is slow to learn or cowardly, she returns it to the nest, and begins to tear it apart, until there is nothing left for the eaglet to cling to. Then she nudges him off the cliff.

True leaders are not bosses. They grow with their people. They strive to make individuals in the organization or society grow to their full ability. They teach and guide just like the mother eagle does. They never stop giving challenges but never give-up empowering and directing.[26] Peter, and the sons of Zebedee were rural dwellers and had only fishing skills. However, when Christ called them, he trained them, he anointed them, he taught, and preached to them and impacted authority and power onto them. They cast out demons, healed the sick and laid the foundation of the Church. They also became authors of five books of the new Testament. Mathew was a publican who was ostracized by the society but when Christ called him, he made him an apostle, he also trained him to become a gospel writer. Eagle Christians are **good trainers.** They are educators and educationists. They are great political leaders who serve as a role module for future generations. Ronald Reagan serves as a role module for the Republican Party. Abraham Lincoln serves as a spring

---

[26] http://iandabasorihetr.hubpages.com/hub/7-Leadership-Characteristics -of-An-Eagle-That-Man-Should-Learn-From (Accessed on August 26, 2013).

board for emancipation of blacks from the shackles of slavery, and a great leader who forsaw the peaceful end of the civil war. Great leaders are eagle Christians. They usher nations and kingdoms into economic boom. Bill Clinton eight-year leadership as the president of the United States ushered in economic boom for Americans. The marginalized blacks and Hispanic speaking populations were given lucrative jobs whose standards of living escalated above normal. Eagle Christians will rescue the masses from economic enslavement.

## EAGLES NEVER EAT DEAD MEAT

The eagle is not a vulture or a scavenger that depends on carcass for survival. The eagle is an avaricious and unconquerable bird. The eagle is not poor and does not eat leftovers of other people's diner. He is financially sufficient, and he hunts for the right jobs, and finds the right people. The eagle Christian avoids junk food. Some sexual relations are junk sex. Some human relations are junk relationships. The eagle hunts for the prey while it is warm and alive. As a leader, you must go to where the action is. You must go and hunt down and find lively people to grow your business. If you are into movie business, go to Hollywood and sell out your business to people who can help you. If you are into kingdom business, go to the right Christian organizations, Churches, pastors and bishops who will recognize your talents and make it great for you. If you are into education, work with District or State department of Education to fulfill your dreams and goals. Sell out your business on the internet, magazines, Tv ads, and media that will embrace your vision and dreams.[27] Eagles do not eat carcasses of their neighborhood.

---

[27] http://thealphanetworkeralliance.com/personal-development/you-must-possess-the-seven-leadership-characteristics-of-an-eagle/(Accessed on August 26,2013)

# Prayer opens Your Spiritual Eyes and Authenticates Your Vision

Prayer is the barometer by which God opens your spiritual eyes and endows you with divine vision. When you pray, the imagination of your mind's eye is illuminated and given direction in life. When divine direction is bestowed upon you, your goals, dreams, and visions are accomplished. While the watching world saw the ultimate defeat in the shame of the cross, Jesus saw a towering victory over Satan and beyond the cross, emanating life in God's eternal kingdom for all who would follow him. The book of Hebrews tells us that he endured the cross "for the joy set before him" so that the vision of the victory that his suffering has accomplished.

The second aspect is that prayer would empower you to deliver your most cherished speeches, goals and dreams of life. Prayer rescued Hezekiah from the jaws of death and extended his life for a decade and half. Prayer rescued Daniel from the den of ferocious lions. Prayer extricated shadrack, Meshack, and Abednego from high voltage furnace. Prayer rescued Jonah from the belly of a fish. Prayer recued Paul and silas from a Roman jail. Corporate prayer rescued the chief apostle, peter from the inner cell of a Roman jail. Prayer is the means by which you can be rescued from every perilous circumstance of your life. It is a magnetic force used to solve every problem. Even on the cross, Jesus defeated Satan by declaring, "It is finished."

Former president John F. Kennedy aligning himself with the American vision, and dream made a powerful statement. It was a memorable challenge. He stated,

> *"I believe that this nation should commit itself to achieving a goal before this decade is out, of landing a man on the moon and returning him safely to earth."*

Must we not pray? Prayer involves powerful statements and speeches that emanate from heaven. Prayer is a fuel that ignites your goals, dreams, and visions into an invincible driving force. As the president made a powerful speech accompanied with the faith of the heart, the mind and faith of the eye, his dream was realized. In addition, in 1969, America was able to send two astronauts to the moon. Positive statements accompanied with faith in God produce a bumper harvest of undeniable achievements. His dream and vision for America was materialized even after his death.

President Ronald Reagan with a spectacular manifestation of a faith enshrined in the word of God and accompanied by a strong will, strong goal, absolute, and a zealous dream, made a powerful statement.

Standing before the long Brandenburg Gate and the Berlin wall in 1987, he declared, *"This wall will fall." Beliefs become reality, "you, across Europe, this wall will fall. For it cannot withstand faith. It cannot withstand truth. The wall cannot withstand freedom."*

Just as the Jericho wall came tumbling down by faith and obedience to God, accompanied with anointed prayer, trumpeting and in the guidance of Joshua and YAHWEH, the Berlin wall was crushed in 1989. Two years after the president made such a powerful prayer, the wall could not withstand prayer and faith. Your prayer accompanied with faith solves seemingly difficult problems. Impossibilities become possibilities. Enemies are overcome, defeated and crushed out of life like chaff. Do you want to succeed? Then pray. Thus, the wall that separated communist East Berlin from the democratic West came down in 1989, paving a glorious way for democracy to prevail in the entire German state. It brought about tranquility, peace and harmony in Germany, in Europe and in the world.

Benjamin Franklin states, "Sunday being my studying day, I never was without some religious principles. I never doubted, for instance, the existence of the Deity; that He made the world, and governed it by His providence; that the most acceptable service of God was the doing good to man; that our souls are immortal; and that all crime will be punished, and virtue rewarded, either here or hereafter." Thus, great inventors, and icons believe in the existence of God and make statements about God that made them invincible.

# Prayer Rescues you from the Lions' Den (Dan 6:1-28)

Prayer has the effectiveness to recue you from the Lion's Den. It has divine miraculous power to extricate you from the grip of malicious, tyrant, atrocious, mischievous, callous, and bloodthirsty people and leaders. With Christocentric prayer as well as Elohistic OR Theo-centric prayer, the enemy is destined to be crushed out of life. What appears to be impossible will become possible when you engage in Christocentric prayer. An archetype of God salvaging a godly personality in the Bible is enshrined in the apocalyptic book of Daniel 6:1-28. **Daniel** דָּנִיֵּאל)) is transcribed as *Daniyyel* and in Tiberian it is *Dāniyyêl*,meaning in Hebrew "God is my Judge. The king of Persia planned to make ministerial appointment so that the empire could experience economic boom as well as receive formidable and invincible protection from the king and its leadership. He was to appoint 120 satraps, and 3 administrators. The satraps were the wise living in the Persian Kingdom. They were the economic experts, business professionals, political connoisseurs, legal and judiciary specialists, immigration experts, and Tax authorities. They also included military connoisseurs. They were the ones who wielded leadership dexterity in the kingdom. Their decision was a matter of urgency and the king had to act on it. They were the ones who mounted pressure on the king to accept some political and national findings and decisions. They persuaded the king to accept some diabolical decisions so that an edict could be passed on them. They were undoubtedly wise, but they were very wicked at certain times.

Nevertheless, there was a holy spirit-filled young, energetic man full of wisdom living in exile in the Persian Kingdom. His name was Daniel. Daniel had exceptional qualities in that he so distinguished himself among the 120 satraps, and the 3 administrators. Having displayed admirable and exceptional qualities, the king planned "to set him over the whole kingdom" (Dan. 6:3).The satraps and administrators welled-up with jealousy, envy and wickedness, and witch-hunted him. They tried to find false with him in the matters of government affairs and the laws of the Land. They were tyrants. They breathed out venom and planned to execute him by crude means. Their plans failed miserably and woefully to yield diabolical dividends. Daniels was found to be law-abiding and a good citizen. He "was trustworthy and neither corrupt nor negligent" (Dan. 6:4). In the kingdom of God, the sovereign God will always deliver those who are trustworthy. He will always deliver those who trust him and depend on him for deliverance. Another quality about Daniel was that he was not **negligent.** He did not derelict his duties. He did not plunge himself into apostasy. He was law-abiding, hardworking and full of wisdom. In addition, because of his commitment to God, they tried to use his worship of God to entrap him, mesmerize him, judge him in a kangaroo court, and lynch him prematurely. Another quality about Daniel was that he was not **corrupt.** According to the *American Heritage Dictionary,* **corrupt** is defined as **marked by immorality and perversion, to ruin morally, to destroy or subvert the honesty or integrity of, or to ruin utterly in character or quality.** So Daniel was not destroyed in character, he was not stained in his moral lifestyle with the state and God. His integrity was intact and they could not find any false with him.

They devised a plan to entrap him in the worship of the God of Israel. The satraps, administrators, advisers, governments, and prefects summoned themselves before the king and exhorted him to issue an edict preventing the worship of all Gods except the god of Persia, who was the king himself. Anyone who refused to worship the king **only,** would be thrown into the lion's den so that the lions could have a sumptuous human meal for the day. The enemy had devised a plan that could terminate the life of Daniel prematurely. He was to be devoured by ravenous lions. He was to be torn into piece and shared among the male lions, female lions, and the cubs. The most hungry amongst them would have crushed his head before he reached the bottom of the den. Since the council of elders, or cabinet ministers, or the FBI or Secret service had devised a plan against Daniel, the king issued an edict forbidding the worship of all gods. Whosoever did so, did it to their own risk. "Now, O king, issue the decree and put it in writing so that it cannot be altered-In accordance with the laws of the Medes and Persians, which cannot be repealed. So king Darius put the decree in writing" (Dan. 6:8).

Another significant quality of Daniel was that he knew how to use information. The use of right information is bound to increase productivity. Receiving the right information and using it appropriately will extricate you from danger and premature death. Using the right information via conversation, radio, Television set, Internet or through electronic media will salvage you from a myriad of problems. Scripture categorically states, *"When Daniel **learned** that the degree had been published, he went home to his upstairs room where the windows opened toward Jerusalem. Three times a day he got down on his knees and prayed, giving thanks to God, just as he had done before"*(Dan. 6:10).

The American Heritage Dictionary defines information as **knowledge derived from study, experience or instruction.** It is also described as **knowledge of specific events or situations that has been gathered or received by communication.** Therefore, Daniel had a wealth of information about events and situations in the kingdom regarding the worship of Elohim and the worship of other gods. He had information that they wanted to entrap him in the worship of the God of Israel. The King James Version states, **"When Daniel knew that the writing was signed" (Dan. 6:10a).** **Knowledge** means state or fact of knowing. Familiarity, awareness, or understanding gained through experience or study. Daniel had collected facts about their wicked decision to assassinate him. Having done his studies, and having had enough statistical data concerning the tyrannical decision orchestrated and perpetrated against him, he took an **action.** People who act on the right information are bound to succeed. People who act on information based on **economics, business ideas, government policies, and social norms** are destined to become leaders and millionaires. People, who act on the right information, would avoid the assassinations plans of gangsters, criminals, rogues, vandals, barbarians and wicked leaders.

The **first plan of action** was to pray, giving thanks to his God.

Prayer is a magnetic force that turns the face of God in your favor but decimates the kingdom of Satan and your enemies. Prayer is more potent than a nuclear warhead. It carries tons and tons of chemical and biological missiles capable of destroying every satanic plan, kingdom, and territory while at the same time ushering you into prosperity and making you to possess the Land. Abraham and Sarah prayed and God gave them Isaac. David prayed and called on God in order to overcome Goliath, the philistines, the Amalekites, the Jebusites Mideanites, the Moabites, and the Perizzites. Prayer makes you a spiritual army General. Prayer makes you the John Calvin or John Westley of your time. It makes you the Augustine of your time. Prayer energizes you to become the Abraham Lincoln of your time. Prayer makes you a champion and not a loser. Prayer will make you a conqueror and not a loser. Prayer will make you the Aquinas, the John Wycliffe, the Kenneth Pike of your time. Prayer has the ability to give you leadership skills of Jesus, Peter and Paul. You will become the Ronald Reagan, the Theodore Roosevelt, and Woodrow Wilson of your time. Prayer will catapult you from commonness into making you a champion in your endeavors. With prayer, you are destined to win every battle. Moses prayed in the wilderness and overcame the Amalekites. He prayed and acted and water gushed out of a stone. He prayed and God relented from pouring his wrath on the stiff-necked people when they worshipped the golden calf. Prayer saves, delivers, and prospers you. Elisha prayed and received a double portion of Elijah's anointing. Elijah cried to God and received a sumptuous meal from quails.

Therefore, Daniel cried to God in the upper room when he learned that the edict was published with the intention of lynching him. He was a prayer warrior because he prayed three times in a day. Even though he was in a foreign land whose citizens worshipped pagan gods and abhorred the God of Israel, Daniel still prayed three times in a day. You cannot pray and remain the same. You cannot pray and fail to have divine answers. You cannot pray and remain in the lion's den. God is great and his mercies endure forever. While he was praying, a grouped of men who vehemently opposed him, witch-hunted him.

They saw him praying and it was immediately reported to the king. Why? They were jealous and begrudging of Daniel's accomplishment and moral impeccable lifestyle. He was an epitome of moral perfection in the kingdom. He constituted the zenith of leadership skills in the kingdom. Scripture categorically asserts, *"Then these men went as a group and found Daniel praying and asking for help"*(Dan. 6:11). Daniel asked God for help. If you ask for help, all conspirators will be defeated. If you ask for help, the Lord will send forth his angelic host to rescue you. Ask God daily for help.

Obviously, Daniel was thrown into the lion's den and " **a stone was brought and placed over the mouth of the den, and the king sealed it with his own signet ring and with the rings of his nobles, so that Daniel's situation might not be changed" (Dan 6:17).**

The king's signet ring used to seal the den meant that the death sentence imposed on Daniel by the method of rapacious lions' **consumption** could not be changed. The **signet** ring in this context was a **symbol** of authority. He was to be gulped by angry, marauding, powerful lions. The nobles were next in rank in the Persian Empire. They wielded the **authority** to exonerate a culprit or find him guilty. Their signet rings were also used to seal the lion's den after Daniel was thrown into it. It meant that it was a collective decision taken by the power structure of the empire. Who can rescue you under such a wicked decision? Mind you, Daniel was a foreigner, with foreign accent, with different lifestyle but obeyed the laws of the Medes and the Persians. His fellow Israelites lived in captivity. They were subjected to hard labor. He had no relative to support him. As usual, he had no access to an attorney, no access to the mayor, no access to those who really could come to his aid. He was left without human consolation, no encouragement, no leadings and no help whatsoever. He was rejected, even though nobody in the Persian kingdom wielded wisdom and anointing like him. The people were ungodly, whose hearts and minds were governed by the gods of this earth. They had no sympathy what so ever. Nevertheless, Daniel knew what to do in times of imminent danger. He resorted to Christocentric prayer. He prayed to God for help and God actually rescued him.

Furthermore, the king in a traumatic mood called at dawn to find out whether Daniel was still alive. Daniel answered, *"O King, live forever! My God sent his angel and he shut the mouths of the lions. They have not hurt me, because I was found innocent in his sight. Nor have I ever done any wrong before you, O King"* (Dan 6:21-22).

Prayer provokes angelic visitation. It ensures you of the arrival of divine rescue team. A versatile angelic-general arrived as soon as he was thrown into the den to help him. Our God is a miraculous personality. When the Egyptian hotly pursued the Israelites and Moses called on God, their archenemies drowned while they escaped. Our God performs unfathomable miracles for us when we feel left alone, betrayed or treated unfairly or when justice is blatantly denied. God rescues the godly from the jaws of avaricious lions and carnivores. You will not die prematurely if you call on the God of the Universe, the creator of heavens and earth. Daniel was pulled out of the lion's den and those who falsely accused him were rather thrown into the den along with their wives and children. *"Before they reached the floor of the den, the lions overpowered them and crushed all their bones"* (Dan 6:24b). Prayer crushes your enemies. Prayer disgraces every opponent and decimates their moral integrity. Prayer has the ability to demolish every thought that sets itself against the knowledge of God. If you understand the theological and biblical wealth of Daniel chapter six, all those who are against your progress, wealth acquisition and prosperity will be crushed. Those who want you to die prematurely will rather die. You have the ability to demolish ungodly nations and territories. You are destined to conquer, live long and enjoy life.

## A CALL FOR COOPERATE PRAYERS IN TIMES OF CRISIS

Second Chronicles 20, is a paradigm of the effectiveness and power of cooperate prayers. Faced with the greatest crisis of his life as the King of Judah, Jehoshaphat met ostensibly impracticable situation in a commendable style. As a king who knows what to do in times of emergency, he immediately began to seek the Lord through fasting and prayer. He gathered the entire Judah to join forces with him in seeking the Lord. Jehoshaphat based his prayer and confidence in God on five principle truths.

1. God has power over all people and situations
- God has been faithful to his people in the past and present
- God's people are helpless without him
- God's promises are a sure foundation for faith
- God's active presence among his people means deliverance and victory.

As they praised God in songs, in the face of a battle, they became victorious. Cooperate prayer opens the gates of heaven to rescue his people in times of difficulties and life battles. When Christians are united in prayer, fighting the enemy with prayer and the word of God, it makes it easy to overcome him. Just as it takes a team to win a soccer match or a basketball game, so it takes, a team of prayer warriors to subdue what may appear seemingly impossible in the eyes of man.

If Jehoshaphat and the entire Israel had given up the enemy would have made booty out of the nation of Israel.

Acts of the Apostles, chapter 12 is one of the heartbreaking stories that the early Church, especially leaders of the time faced. At the birth of Jesus, Jews encountered severe persecutions by the then wicked king of the Roman Empire, King Herod. He committed Genocidal acts against the children of Israel at the time Mary gave birth to Jesus. He slaughtered many male children and tried to lynch Jesus since he was a threat to him. After his death, his son Herod Antipas decapitated the Apostle James in the first paragraph of Acts chapter 12. He was still breathing out venom against the Church by arresting Peter, the leader of the Church and imprisoning him. Nevertheless, valiant Church members gathered at the house of Mary to seek the face of God for the deliverance of the super apostle.

Through their unrelenting prayer that rose up like incense to God, an angel of the Lord visited him in the inner cell of the prison and extricated him from the shackles of imprisonment. In the Roman Empire, the inner cell constituted a dungeon of punishment. Culprits or inmates were severely flogged and brutalized. The chief apostle was put in a precarious cell where the prison guards might have flogged him severely. Nevertheless, the divine personality led him out of the prison until he realized that he was rescued from the slaughter of the wicked King Herod. While believers were still groaning and prevailing in prayer for the release of Peter, he knocked at the door of the house where believers gathered to intercede for him. Rhoda, a little girl announced to the group the miraculous arrival of Peter. Peter narrated his escape from prison to the staunch believers of the Lord. They beheld the miracle of God with prayer.

Cooperate prayer is more potent than biological warheads. Cooperate prayer is capable of diffusion surface-to-surface spiritual missile of any kind. When you gather as true believers of God to pray, miracles occur. Do not forsake the assembly of the brethren (Heb. 10:25), for doing so you will reap both earthly and heavenly harvest.

## PRAYER OF CONFESSION

There are times that you must pray confessing your sins. In Proverbs 28: 13, the lesson of confession of sin or transgression is formulated as follows: *"He who conceals his transgressions will not prosper; he who confesses and forsakes them will obtain mercy.* To obtain mercy from the sovereign God, who is the author and finisher of your faith, you definitely need his mercies and steadfast love. In addition, to obtain this, you need to confess your sins believing that he will forgive you. Confessing of sin also delivers you from torment. You certainly need to confess your sins to eschew torment. For example, in Psalm 32: 3-5, the Psalmist tells about the torment he suffered when he was silent and the forgiveness he received when he acknowledged his sin to the Lord. David made a typical confession of sin in Psalm 51 after Prophet Nathan confronted him with his adulterous relationship with Bathsheba. David's confession of sin is based on the grace of God. He says, "Be gracious to me". He appeals for God's steadfast love and mercy. David had deep and earnest desire to be reinstated to a cordial relationship with God. His confession is based on divine grace that establishes a firm and right relationship with God. His appeal for divine grace is based on God's attribute of being "merciful". The word is crowning act of genuine and abiding love. "Tender mercies" refer to parental affection. He appeals to God to wash him thoroughly of his sins and to cleanse him so that he can shine. He acknowledges that it is only God he has sinned against. He asks God to purify him and make him hear joy and gladness. This indicates that we should not adopt a holier than thou attitude when we fall into sin but must earnestly plead for the forgiveness of God. . The word "confession" in the New Testament is taken from the Greek word (**homologeo**), meaning *"to cite"*, *"to name"*, *"to classify in the same manner"* *"to agree with"*, *"to say the same thing as"*. We must admit our sins and seek forgiveness and purifying from God. Confession acknowledges God's rulership in the matter and agrees with His judgment.

Furthermore, the Greek word for "merciful" is *eleemon*, which implies executing generous deeds of deliverance. Mercy is a generous action that engages in delivering someone else from trouble or bondage. It reaffirms proverbs 14:21, which declares, "He who despises his neighbor sins, but blessed is he who is kind to the needy." Nevertheless, mercy in the gospel depicts forgiveness that rescues from the bondage of guilt. It is an action that heals and gives freedom to the needy. According to Luis Berkhof, "it is the goodness or love of God shown to those who are in misery or distress, irrespective of their deserts."[28] He further affirms that the Hebrew word used most often to refer to mercy is *chased*. Another word frequently used in the Bible is *richen,* which is rendered tender mercies in

---

[28] Luis Berkhof, *Systematic Theology* (Grand Rapids, Michigan/Cambridge, UK: William B. Eerdmans, 1996), 72

English Language.[29] His mercy is depicted as God revealing himself as a compassionate God, who has insatiable love for those who are engrossed in misery. He is ever ready to alleviate them from their anguish. His mercy is plentiful (Deut 5:10; Ps 57:10; 86:5).

In the Lord's Prayer Jesus employs a different word for forgiveness, *aphiemi* (Mt 6:12), which might have been translated from an Aramaic verb connoting, "to forgive." When the two blind men called out to Jesus saying, "Have mercy on us son of David" (Mt 9:27), they meant "heal us, deliver us from our affliction." It is for the same reason that Mt 6: 2 executing merciful acts, *eleemosyne*, implies giving alms to the poor. Actually, the Gospel of Matthew dilates so much on mercy. It is a fundamental demand (Mt 9: 13; 12:7; 23:23). The disposition of mercy towards the needy could not be glossed over by Jesus. For, mercy requires an outward act and an inward feeling for the oppressed, the out casts, the down trodden, and the sinners. It is acknowledged as a human virtue and a divine attribute. Jesus opponents neglected important virtues such as "justice", "mercy", and "faith" (Mt 23:23). Accordingly, merciful deeds are concrete loyalty to God, benefiting others as the loving kindness of God.[30]

Confession of sin looks beyond self to God and lays hold on the marvelous possibilities of God's grace. Those who confess their sin know and believe that God judges their life. For you to have your prayer answered, you have to humbly submit yourself to God by confessing your inadequacies, weakness and above all your transgressions to him. To survive in this perilous world, we undeniably need the love and mercies of God. We can achieve this through prayer.

Growing up in a culture where respect for elders and one another is placed on a high premium of the social structure, a good mark of an obedient child is not to make mistakes or err, but the ability for the child to acknowledge his wrong and then plead for forgiveness. As soon as he confesses his sins, he is accepted back, loved, and

---

[29] Ibid., 72.

[30] Glen H. Stassen & David P. Gushee: *Kingdom Ethics* (Downers Grove, Illinois: Intervarsity Press, 2003), 43.

cherished by parents and the community. Our God is beyond the people of this culture. God is willing and ever ready to accept us back. Your duty is to acknowledge your transgressions, sins, and God will accept you back. It does not matter how far you have fallen from the grace of God, he is willing to take you back.

## CONFESSING THE SIN OF NATIONS

One of the most important elements in Christian leadership is acknowledgement of one's transgressions and taking the necessary measures to remedy them. God speaks to us through his word and we in turn communicate with God through prayer. Nehemiah became a man of prayer as he led the post-exilic remnants to build the wall of Jerusalem. Ezra 1-6 expatiates on **rebuilding the Temple.** Under the instruction of God, King Cyrus, the King of Persia assisted the remnants to rebuild the Temple in Jerusalem. Zerubbabel, a Jewish figure in Persia spearheaded the rebuilding of the Temple. Through two formidable prophets, Haggai and Zechariah living in Jerusalem, the Temple was completely restored. Furthermore, rebuilding the Temple meant that their spiritual life was to be reconstructed since Temple worship was abandoned for seventy years. Since most of the Jews had never heard of the Law of Moses, Ezra set off the spiritual rejuvenation exercise by studying the law of God, practicing it and teaching it (Ezra 7-10).

Even though the Temple was restored, and stood up as the most beautiful and dominant structure in Jerusalem, the walls of the city were still devastated. This was security threat as well as national humiliation since the city was so vulnerable to every form of military invasion. Another zealous and capable Jewish leader serving Artaxerxers, the King of Persian in the person of Nehemiah was burdened to reconstruct the walls of Jerusalem. Permission was granted and within the shortest possible time, he had accomplished the task with the help of the people. He encountered so many ordeals but he used prayer to diffuse tension and to accomplish what God had appointed him to execute. Nehemiah prayed in a storm of emotion, he wept, mourned, and fasted on a number of occasions (Neh 1:4). He prayed asking God to remember what he promised to His servant Moses (Neh 1:8). His acknowledgement of the word of God provoked his faith into action. As a good leader, he confessed the sins of the people including himself.

Daniel follows the same principle, "we have sinned, and we have not listened." The sins were neither Daniel's nor Nehemiah's, and yet in both of these instances, the great prayer warriors identified themselves with the people for whom they were praying. A good leader will identify himself with the people in times of crises to intercede, petition and confess their sins for them.

## PRAYER OF PROTECTION

As a Christian, you need to pray for the protection of God from dangers and attacks from Satan. It is very wise to protect your properties and life from intruders and undesirable elements. People install security cameras, alarm systems in their homes and properties to ward off and to trap those who intend to cause harm to them. In the USA, security cameras, alarm systems, watchdogs or a security guard secures almost every home or building. To add to the above, you need to call on God daily to bring you under the canopy of his protection. He is the ultimate protector. Without his protection, you can be swept away in the twinkle of an eye. The psalmist in Psalm 91 states that God is his refuge. A metaphor used for God's protection and care. In its liturgical context, it means to look to the LORD for security from threatening dangers. The psalmist speaks of God as protector of those who trust in Him. The LORD is referred to as *fortress, stronghold, dwelling place, and shelter.* When you make the Lord your stronghold, nothing can break your ranks. The enemy will throw fiery darts at you but they will not come near you. When LORD becomes your dwelling place, His continuous presence will comfort you, protect, guard, and guide you in your walk with Him. You will be sheltered from the whims, capricious and venomous attacks of the enemy. It is imperative to call on God to protect you from the snare of the fowler, pestilence, lion, udder, evil and to prevent you from dashing your foot against a stone. For example, the psalmist declares, "For in the day of trouble he will keep me safe in his dwelling; he will hide me in the shelter of his tabernacle and set me high upon a rock. Then my head will be exalted above the enemies who surround me" (Ps 27: 5-6a). King David in penning this psalm believed that God could protect him from dangerous situations. He trusted his God in all areas of his life. Psalm 62:1 echoes a similar sentiment, "Only in God does my soul wait in silence, and from him is my salvation."

Furthermore, comprehending the methods and intentions of his adversaries, he called on God to surround him with impregnable protection. He asserts, "You are my hiding place; you will protect me from trouble and surround me with songs of deliverance" (Ps 32:7). Until you pray for divine protection, the enemy will always have an upper hand over your life and property. Until you pray for protection, the adversary will always endeavor to take you by surprise. Praying for protection is biblical and beneficial. David in a similar tone calls on God by declaring, "Do not withhold your mercy from me, O Lord; may your love and truth always protect me" (Ps 40:11). David having faced several perilous situations in his life, continued to pray for his personal protection and for the protection of the nation of Israel until his death at an old age. He states, "Protect me O Lord, from evil men; protect me from men of violence, who devise evil plans in their hearts and stir up war every day. They make their tongue as sharp as a serpent's; the poison of vipers is on their lips. Keep me, O Lord, from the hands of the wicked; protect me from men of violence who plan to trip my feet" (Ps 140:1-4). The believer of the 21st century must ascertain that there are evil people. He must agree and have it firm in his heart that criminals surround us. We have to acknowledge that our lives are in danger, and that evil men and women are vomiting out violence against us. You have to pray against the poisonous tongue of evil and criminal people. You must also pray against men and women of violence, who are prepared to fight you and to lay their evil hands on you.

The gruesome massacre of 33 people in Virginia Tech in 2007, and 20 students, and seven other adults of Sandy Hook Elementary School in Newtown, Connecticut on December 14, 2012 necessitates us to be alert. A few years ago, 15 people in Colobine High School were exterminated via assault rifles and guns. To curb this perennial problem, all security agencies, the police, secret service, teachers, parents, pastors, congressional representatives and women, senators, government officials, and community leaders must collaborate in order to find a workable solution to the slewing of innocent people. Innocent citizens must be protected from such hideous attacks. Apart from enacting laws that will ensure absolute safety of innocuous citizens, Christians must always call on the invincible Lord for protection. Scripture asserts, "The name of the Lord is a strong tower, the righteous run to him and are saved." According to ABC world News, anchored by Dianne Sawyer on December 17, 2012 at 6.30PM pacific standard Time, and 9:30 Eastern standard time, Americans are 20 times more likely to be shot by a gun than people living in other countries. According to ABC news on December 18, 2012, there are about 200 million guns in the hands of private citizens. Some of them wield arms and ammunitions that are created for military for warfare on the battlefield. For instance, Adam Lanza wielded the **bushmaster;** a special assault rifle designed for long range and short-term warfare. In the case of Sandy Hook Elementary School slaughter, the principal, teachers, and six and seven year old children apparently were helpless in the face of this mentally deranged, hysterical and confused armed combatant who cocked up that deadly weapon releasing piercing bullets into them, massacring 26 people, before turning the deadly weapon to himself. Further research has indicated that 15 million American children have a mental disorder problem that is 1 out of five children suffers from mental ailment. For instance, Adam Lanza who executed the 26 people at Sandy Hook Elementary School including himself was psychologically and mentally traumatized, and in 2012, 16

American communities experienced mass shootings. Thirty-four Americans are killed every day by a firearm, which means 12410 people are assassinated annually if we multiply 34 by 365 days. This calls for intensification of prayer for protection from criminals and disgruntled individuals. According to **authoritative study** by the United Nations on **Homicide**, 70% of which guns are used constitutes 15th leading cause of death for the Americans.

# CHAPTER 2

## MAKING TIME TO KNOW GOD-
## THE CONGREGATION

An important aspect of prayer is making time to communicate with God. Moses, the elders, and the congregation had different level of understanding and communication with God. Those encamped at the foot of the mountain experienced God from a distance (Ex 24: 3-8). In Exodus 20, when God spoke with brims ton, light and heavy trumpeting, the people fled from God and stood in a distance (Ex 20:1, 18). They failed to fellowship with God. They watched God from a distance and the intimacy that a covenant people of God were supposed to have with him was virtually missing. Never did they spend long hours basking in his Shekinah. Never did they experience the permeation of God's wonderful transforming power. Never did they long for the beauty of God in His Holy presence. They beheld the fire and glory of God rising from the top of the mountain but they never made an effort to comprehend the source of these supernatural happenings. It was their utmost desire to be alienated from God while Moses acted as a mediator (Ex 24:15-18). Some Christians live most part of their lifetime basking in the misery of the foot of the mountain. After Jesus has saved them, they prefer to watch the glory of the saving power of Jesus in aloofness. They profess they are Christians, and yet they are not spirit-filled. They claim they are tongue-speaking believers, and yet they do not spend ample time with their savior. They see Jesus' glory like the blind man saw people like trees (Mark 8:24). These types of believers see Jesus dimly. They do not experience the happiness and empowerment of the Holy Spirit. They are content with the little encounters they have with Jesus Christ on monthly basis or on Christmas or New Year's Eve. They know the Lord but they have a superficial knowledge of him. They do not meditate the word in their own private studies. As a result, they do not hear the voice of God, they lose the direction of God and God's given dreams, and purposes are lost in their lives.

## MAKING TIME TO KNOW GOD-THE ELDERS

The seventy elders on the other hand attempted to know God better. "Moses and Aaron, Nadab and Abihu, and the seventy elders of Israel went up and saw the God of Israel. Under his feet was something like a pavement made of sapphire, clear as the sky itself. Nevertheless, God did not raise his hand against these leaders of the Israelites; they saw God and they ate and drank (Ex 24: 9-11)." Even though the Elders saw the glory of God, it was very brief. It lasted only a few hours or days. Verses 12 and 13 indicate that God called His servant Moses to the top of the mountain leaving behind the elders at the slope of it. As compared to the **congregation** at the foot of the mountain, they knew God deeper and a special way. This is because they sought God more. Instead of drawing back, they drew closer. Isaiah echoes a similar sentiment when he says, *"seek the Lord while he may be found; call on him while he is near."(Isaiah 55:6)*. They had a firsthand experience with God and not a secondary one. It a direct communication between them and God. Even though they had a firm and intimate relationship with God, it was highly limited in scope as compare to that of Moses who went to the mountaintop.

## Prayer involves listening

Many Christians think that prayer is a one-way traffic whereby they only have to cry to God all the time. It is not so. As we speak to God, we need to provide time to listen to him. Listening is a powerful means of communication; it has the same amount of influence as talking. Lack of concentration and reverential listening can be costly-making way for mistakes, poor service, crooked goals, washed out time and lack of coordination. When God called Ezekiel to go and speak to the post-exilic people, he instructed him to listen to him. "Son of man, listen carefully and take heart all the words I speak to you" (Ezek. 3:10). He was to stand in contrast to the remnants that were obstinate to the instruction of God. Proverbs 1: 5 states "let the wise listen and add to their learning". When God called the Prophet Samuel, Eli the High priest instructed him to respond to God by saying, "speak Lord, for your servant is listening" (1Sam 3:9). Every Christian needs to ask God to speak to them. In the New Testament, the brother of Jesus says, "everyone should be quick to listen, slow to speak and slow to become angry" (James 1:19). Every Christian must master the art of listening, for it is an effective way of communicating to others. It is not only in business ethics, family meetings, and social clubs that we must nurture the habit of listening but the most important of all is to develop the skill of listening to God.

King David, the man found to be after God's owns heart and author of most Psalms knew how to listen to God. In the morning, he sought the face of God before embarking on the day's activities. *"Let the morning bring me word of your unfailing love, for I have put my trust in you. Show me the way I should go, for to you, I lift up my soul (Psalm 143:8).* He sought the direction of God for his life before getting on any project. David reechoes a similar tone in Psalm 5: 3 "In the morning, *"O Lord, you hear my voice; in the morning I lay my requests and wait in expectation.*

# Mary listened to Jesus

*"As Jesus and his disciples were on their way, he came to a village where a woman named Martha, opened her home to him. She had a sister called Mary, who sat at the Lord's feet listening to what he said. But Martha was very distracted by all the preparations that had to be made."(Luke 10:38-40).*

Most Christians are so busy and are distracted by so many events in their lives. We are busy working, busy making money, busy holdings meetings, busy attending services, busy going to the movies, busy watching TV, busy on the internet, busy talking or chatting away our time so that there is no time left to listen to Jesus. Martha was such a Christian. She devoted most of her time to prepare for the arrival of Jesus to the extent that she forgot to listen to words of life from him. She was possibly busy cooking, washing dishes, cleaning the house, pressing clothing and possible decorating the house with the finest flowers. It is even possible she sprayed the house with an alabastron perfume, an **expensive** fragrance during the time of Jesus an equivalent of post- modern day Clive Christian imperial majesty perfume. In addition, the house might have been sprayed with frankincense and myrrh in the anticipation of Jesus arrival. As a result, she missed the most precious aspect of Jesus' visit to their home.

Mary the sister of Martha did the opposite. She chose to listen to Jesus instead of devoting much of her time to inconsequential issues. It is better to listen to the words of salvation from the savior himself than to have the house filled with evanescent food. It is far rewarding to spend time imbibing the words of Jesus and taking instructions from Him than to be engaged in events that have little spiritual reward. In the sixth chapter of the Gospel of John, the verse 63, Jesus states, "The Spirit gives life, the flesh counts for nothing. The words I have spoken to you are spirit and they are life." No philosopher or any think thank can challenge the words of Jesus Christ. His words are rewarding, healing, comforting and they are therapeutic in perspective. If you cultivate the habit of listening to Jesus, you will grow to be a mature and unshakable personality in the Kingdom of God.

## A PRAYER SATURATED WITH
## FAITH MOVES MOUNTAINS

Faith, which is an expression of absolute confidence, gives an enormous reward in the end. For example, the Lord spoke to Abraham after he had waited 25 years for the fulfillment of the birth of Isaac. To his amazement, God requested Abraham to sacrifice the promised son to him. Sacrifice in the Old Testament was regarded a symbol of worship to God. It indicated a complete trust and faith in God. Abraham believed God, and by that act of faith, he became the father of all who are born again and have an inheritance in God (Rom 4: 3, 10). Faith is an action, and there is no evidence of faith without an act. An action is the authentic evidence of faith. Faith is counterfeit without the back-up action.

Prayer that is not backed by Faith is unproductive. Just as a car is incapable of moving without gasoline or electrically charged, so a prayer offered to God without an iota of Faith makes little impact. The writer of Hebrews clearly states, *"And without faith it is impossible to please God, because anyone who comes to Him must believe that he exists and that he rewards those who earnestly seek him"* (Heb. 11:6). According to the American Heritage Dictionary, *impossible* is *"incapable of having existence or of occurring. Not capable of being accomplished."* In African traditional religion, the faithful believe that the ancestors, gods, and spirits are the supernatural beings. They believe that certain actions will provoke either blessings or curses on them and their belief system works for them even though it is a false faith. Our God is more than any god or ancestor. When he commands us to believe in Him, let us do so. Many a people want to have their prayers answered but fail to trust him to do what he has promised to do. Jesus clearly states in Matthew 17: 20 *"because you have so little faith, I tell you the truth, if you have faith as small as a mustard seed, you can say to this mountain, move from here to there' and it will move. Nothing will be impossible for you."* Prayer that is bathed in faith is bound to produce good results. Scholars have unanimously agreed that the mustard seed was not the smallest seed but it was used to represent smallness in our dealings with God. In some instances, Jesus requested faith from the down trodden and the sick before they could receive their healing and miracles. In Matthew 9:22, *"He said, your faith has healed you."* In Matthew 9: 29 *"He said to the two blind men, according to your faith will it be done."* Then in the same Matthew 21: 21 he says, *"If you believe, you will receive whatever you ask for in prayer."* Any time you request God to accomplish certain things for you, he requires at least a little amount of faith from you. You cannot receive much without faith. With faith, mountainous problems will be uprooted out of your life.

With a little amount of faith, you will make unfathomable progress in your life. Nevertheless, prayer without Faith is like trying to build a house without a foundation. It is also compared to trying to write a PhD dissertation when you have not even started elementary school. Prayer a lone without faith is like rolling an empty drum, it only makes noise, and actually, it has little value. So many Christians are noisemakers. They pray in tongues all day without Faith. Faith is the magnetic force that propels the hand of God to answer our prayers.

Hebrews chapter 11 is an incredible chapter you can discover several reasons to feel mighty fine because you have faith in a God who never disappoints. In this chapter, the writer of Hebrews has clearly pointed out to all believers what faith is and what it can do for us. The chapter demonstrates the only kind of faith acceptable before God, a faith triumph in the worst of situations. It is a faith that believes in spiritual realities, that leads to righteousness, seeks God, believes in his goodness, has confidence in his word, and obeys his commands. If it is an all-important object, then we need to know what it is in the actual sense. It makes living so colorful, and then we must be bothered and concerned about what it is. Nothing works without it. Salvation is impossible without it. Victory is impossible without it. In addition, Christianity is worthless without faith.

What then is Faith? The author of Hebrews clearly points out in verse one that **"Faith is being sure of what we hope for and certain of what we do not see" (Heb.11:1).** Consequently, we must do all we can to make our lives colorful by having unwavering faith in the Lord.The word "faith", translated from the Greek πιστις (*pi'stis*), is employed in the **_New Testament_** with the Greek perfect tense and translates as a noun-verb hybrid. The verbal denotation of *pi'stis* is *pisteuo*, which is translated as 'believe'. The adjectival form, *pistos*, is rendered as 'faithful'. In both the New Testament and other Greek texts, *pi'stis* describes connections of *firmness* that can form between wide varieties of entities: people, traditions, practices, groups, purposes, facts or propositions. The suitable English rendition is often portrayed from the relationship between the two entities connected by *pi'stis*. The *pi'stis*-group words in the New Testament can thus be interpreted as relating to ideas of faithfulness, fidelity, loyalty, commitment, trust, belief, and proof. Thus, the believer is enjoined to stay connected firmly to Jesus in demonstrating fidelity in their relationship with Him. Therefore, if you are faithful or loyal to him, then you are bound to receive abundant blessings in miraculous proportions.

Concisely, prayer involves unflinching Trust in God. In dealing with the Psalms of Trust, it is discovered that this group of psalms makes a strong declaration of their unbending trust in the LORD but fail to always illuminate the occasion that precipitated the statement of absolute confidence. They usually provide clues. Psalm 27 for instance refers to some combative circumstances, which contributed to building up the psalmist confidence in the Lord. "Though an army besieges me, my heart will not fear." (V 3). Psalm 23 in a similar dimension, portrays the psalmist encompassed by a multitude of enemies. "You prepare a table before me in the presence of my enemies" (V 5). Seemingly, difficult circumstances of this nature compelled the psalmists to put their confidence in the Lord. These psalms according to the writer are the expressions of faith, and not crisis of victory. He declares, "Along the landscape of their lives one may see the banners of faith flying above the adversaries." Faith therefore plays a pivotal role in the Psalms of trust. The psalms of trust are classified into individual and community. Those that depict an absolute individual trust in the Lord are 4, 16, 23, 27, 62, and 73. In addition, those that portray the community's trust in the Lord are psalms 90, 115, 123, 124, 125, and 126.

# Prayer and Understanding the Word of God will make you a Wise person

Prayer undoubtedly would make you a wise person. It is only a wise personality, who runs to the most powerful person for refuge in times of trouble. It is only a wise person who consorts together with a personality who is an embodiment of wisdom. God is all-powerful, all-wise, and all-knowing. According to scholars, wisdom Psalm conceptualizes life and faith and are best explained in the Books of proverbs, Job, and Ecclesiastes. Two forms of identifications are presented in the wisdom Books. The first is the employment of proverbs abundantly used in the Book of proverbs and is known as proverbial wisdom. "The proverb represents a concentrated expression of the truth." It teaches the truth because it is the tip of the iceberg but teaches volumes of veracity. Thus, "a gossip betrays a confidence, but a trustworthy man keeps a secret" (Prov 11: 13). It requires some little effort and reflection to discern the meaning of the concentrated truth. The second aspect of wisdom, the kind represented by job and the Book of Ecclesiastes is a reflective one. It is reflective because it presents problems that emanates from a veritable life situation. These types of proverbs do not have the answers handy like the proverbial wisdom. It requires higher wisdom than getting the answers unexpectedly. For example, when job friends insisted that the wicked suffers but the righteous prospers, Job vehemently objected to it, using himself as an example of a righteous man, and yet had to go through harrowing times.

Pertaining to the description of Wisdom psalms, the most distinguishing characteristic is the proverb. Psalms 37 displays arrays of proverbs, which are in semblance of the Book of proverbs. "Do not fret because of evil men or be envious of those who do wrong". The second prevailing feature of wisdom literature is admonitions or teachings, most of the time taken from nature. Psalm 37:9, for instance admonishes the Christian not to "be like the horse or the mule, which have no understanding." The third unique feature of the wisdom literature is the employment of similes, usually introduced by "like" or "as". The blessing of children in psalm 128 is a typical example of the use of similes. "Your wife will be like a fruitful vine within your house; your sons will be like olive shoots around your table." (V.3). The fourth attribute of wisdom literature is the "Blessed" (oshri) formula. This formula occurs in psalms 1.1; 34 8b; 112:1b; 127:5; 128:1. It is a method of pronouncing God's endorsement of a scrupulous manner of life or deed. The fifth quality is the teacher's address to his student to take heed of certain behaviors, usually in the form of "sons" or "children". The sixth and final form is the "better" pronouncement, which weights the value of one thing or action over the other. Indubitable example is psalm 37:16, which declares, "Better the little that the righteous have than the wealth of many wicked."

Over the years, I have come to acknowledge that the more I pray and use the word of God appropriately, the more I become wise. This is because prayer will lead you to unearth wisdom principles of God. God is an embodiment of wisdom, so if you run to him in prayer he will not withhold his manifold wisdom from you. James asserts, "If any of you lacks wisdom, he should ask God, who gives generously to all without finding fault, and it will be given to him" (James 1:5). You see, prayer will split open the Eldorado of wisdom for you. Until you go to God asking for wisdom, you will remain a fool. Wisdom will equip you with practical discernment. Practical discernment leads to right living and the ability to discern between wrong and right. Practical discernment will usher you into making right choices. Right choices with God's help leads to high-level productivity and self-actualization. Self-actualization leads to success, growth and advancement.

## PRAYER, FAITH AND HOPE

*"Now faith is the substance of things hoped for..."*
**(Hebrews 11:1)**

Faith undoubtedly engenders hope. Hope comes by the Word, so also faith comes by the Word. However, it takes faith, fertilized by hope, for results to be delivered. Faith gives substance to your hope. To be hopeless is to be helpless! Every time you give up on an issue, you become hopeless. Not even God can help you then, **because without faith, it is impossible to please Him**. No matter how strong your faith is, without hope it is unproductive. Have you ever found a man, no matter how strong he is, who gave birth to children without a woman? Faith gives substance to hope - there is a fertilization that produces eventual evidence. Therefore, if there is no hope, faith has no value! There are quite a lot of people operating at the frequency of hopelessness, yet they are expecting faith to produce. Faith minus hope is barren! What faith does is to fertilize hope. Wherever there is no hope, faith is worthless. Hope is the mother of the evidence that faith produces. When hope is dead, faith is valueless. There is nothing you cannot see coming that will ever come. I am glad to let you know though, **that if you are born again, by destiny you will never get to a point of hopelessness in any area of your life.** You have that assurance in Ecclesiastes 9:4:*"For to him that is joined to all the living there is hope: for a living dog is better than a dead lion."* There is hope for anyone joined to the living God, in whatever situation he might find himself. Hope is what makes faith productive and dynamic, and places the results you are expecting in your hands.

Look at Abraham's case: Despite all odds, Abraham believed! When it was no longer sensible to have hope, Abraham still believed! See how the Bible described it. *"Who against hope believed in hope..."*It is simply amazing! Abraham was not weak in faith. Friends, do you know what hope does? It strengthens your faith! Now concerning that situation, I tell you, "It is not over. This cannot just be the end! Until I win, nobody will blow the final whistle." Hope strengthens faith. *"And being not weak in faith, because he believed in hope"*, the Bible says Abraham considered not his own body, which was as good as dead. As long as you have hope, your faith will remain alive.

## Faith has great recompense of reward (Heb. 11: 6)

Those who have faith in God are rewarded. It is pointed out in verse 6, that *"and without faith it is impossible to please God, because any one who comes to Him must believe that he exists and that he rewards those who earnestly seek Him"* It is by Faith that all Christians come to God. Therefore, when we request anything from Him, he requires us to have absolute Faith in Him. There is nothing beyond the hand of God in it; you only need to have unshakable, unmovable and a formidable faith in God. You may be going through swift currents of life and all that you do may seem like going through a high wave of turbulent period. Have faith in God.

Faith, an expression of confidence, establishes reward- great reward, for instance, the Lord spoke to Abraham, after he had waited 25 years to get Isaac but the Lord asked him to sacrifice his only son to him (paraphrased).

In addition, Abraham set out to do exactly as God had commanded him, believing that God is able to raise sons unto him out of stones (Heb11: 17-19). Abraham believed God, and by that act of faith, he became the father of all those who are born again and have an inheritance with God (Rom. 4:3, 10). Faith is action and therefore there is no evidence of faith without an act. An action is the authentic evidence of faith. Faith is fake without a back-up action.

## Noah's Faith, Samuel and Jesus' favor.

For instance, Noah being warned of God of things not seen as yet, moved with fear, prepared an ark to the saving of his house while the crooked and perverse generation was annihilated by the wrath of God (Heb11: 7). God spoke and Noah moved. Faith compels action. A man with a withered hand came to Jesus and Jesus said, "Stretch forth your hand", and the paralysis disappeared. He acted on faith

DR. DOMINIC NYAABA

and consequently he received his healing. When we act on faith God responds by rewarding us with favor, love, and protection.

In addition to Noah's faith was the fact that he was righteous before God and the people of his time. **"Noah was a righteousness man, blameless among the people of his time, and he walked with God" (Gen. 6:9).** The Hebrew word for righteousness is *tsedagah* meaning "right deeds, right actions, and right thoughts." There is another word that runs parallel to *tsedagah*, which is *mishpat* meaning "justice, administration of justice, bestowal of favor on those who truly deserve it." True faith is seen in righteous deeds and administering of justice to the poor and to those who deserve it. Because of his unflinching faith in God when God spoke to him he listened, he obeyed, he took action based on God's instructions and he was accounted worthy of praise as a man of God, a man of faith, a man of righteous deeds and a man who administered true justice among the people of his time. As a man of faith when God spoke to him, he undertook the construction of the Ark. He obeyed and initiated that project. A man of faith initiates and accomplishes Godly directed projects. While his counterparts were engrossed in uncontrolled sexual promiscuity, Noah's faith in God made him to orchestrate deeds that were counted worthy in heaven and on earth. Because of his faith and righteousness, he, his family, and every kind of animal were saved from a deluge that swept the entire world away. A person imbued with faith will escape the calamities of his time. A person imbued with faith and prayer will escape the inundations of life. A person with Noah's type of faith escapes earthquakes, tornados, hurricanes, and floods of life.

Scripture also states, "But Noah found favor in the eyes of the Lord" (Gen. 6:8). His righteous deeds gave him divine favor. Holy acts will bestow divine favor upon you and your family. Righteous deeds combined with the favor of God will make you escape the virulent sword of judgment. When you have divine favor, you will always escape calamities of life. When you have divine favor, you will always be protected, your family will permanently be protected and you will not die prematurely. The 21$^{st}$ century believer must

64

embrace prayer, coupled with righteous deeds and divine favor in order to unlock miraculous proportions of his or her destiny. Divine prayer will also make you prosperous. You will be prosperous in your businesses, prosperous in your education, prosperous in whatever project you undertake.

Another biblical personality who has been described as receiving God's favor was the boy Samuel. "And the boy Samuel continued to grow in stature and in favor with the Lord and with men" (1 Sam. 2:26). The boy Samuel growing up in the presence of the Lord and ministering before God meant prayer was part of his daily life. So, he grew up in stature and in favor with the Lord, in the presence of God, worshipping, praying and serving his God through Eli, the man of God. Prayer engenders divine favor. Actually, Samuel was attested as the most honorable prophet of God because he spoke the very oracles of God. Thus, a prophet who is prayerful and has divine favor speaks the very oracles of God. A prophet who is imbued with the favor of God is revered by people. Moreover, a person who carries divine favor is honored, respected and appreciated. Scripture attests, "And Jesus grew in wisdom and in stature, and in favor with God and men" (Luke 2:52). Just as Jesus performed miracles, you will perform undeniable miracles if you have the wisdom and favor of God. Just as Jesus performed miracles to the amazement of his disciples and his opponents so will you be a miracle worker. Jesus was invincible in his warfare against Satan and the Pharisees. Prayer will make you dauntless in this century as you unlock your destiny for the manifestation of God's glory. Jesus exhibited fortitude, resilience, excellence, and was outstanding in his messianic calling. You will do likewise in this century if you contend the forces of darkness with prayer. Jesus could not be crucified until his appointed time was due. Prayer will extricate you from the jaws of premature death. On the cross Jesus declared, "It is finished." Prayer will fortify you to deliver a deadly blow to every opposing enemy in every endeavor of your life. On the third day, he resurrected form the dead. Prayer will resurrect your business in this century. Prayer will resurrect your defunct church and congregation. Prayer will make you glorious and flamboyant in your outlook. Just as Jesus is our messiah, prayer, favor and wisdom will give you messianic ideas, messianic hope, messianic projects and messianic breakthroughs. Do you want favor? Prayer is the **key** to divine favor, divine prosperity and divine promotion.

## FAITH IS A PRODUCER OF GOOD REPORTS (HEB. 11:2-35)

Nobody can have a good report without effectually applying faith. Where good reports are found in the kingdom, it is a direct product of faith. Faith is principal determiner of our status. Therefore, every exploit recorded in Heb. 11 is a direct product of faith. By faith Abel offered God a better sacrifice than Cain did (vs. 4), By faith Enoch was taken from this life, so that he did not experience death (5), Abraham obtained good report by faith (vs. 11, 17), By faith Jacob obtained a good report by blessing Joseph's sons (vs. 21), By faith Joseph spoke about the exodus of the Israelites from Egypt and gave instructions about his bones (vs22), By faith Moses parents hid him for three months (vs. 23), By faith Moses refused to be known as the son of, Pharaoh's daughter (vs. 24), By faith the people of Israel passed through the Red sea as on dry land but the Egyptians got drown (vs. 29), By faith the walls of Jericho fell, after the people had marched around them for seven days (vs.30), By faith the prostitute Rehab obtained a good report and was not killed with those who were disobedient (vs.31).

Since good report stems from righteous acts, it affords people the opportunity to perform acts of righteousness. It is pointed out from verses 32-35 that men and women such as Gideon, Barak, Samson, Japhthah, David, Samuel and the prophets through faith conquered kingdoms, administered justice, gained what was promised, who shut the mouths of lions, quenched the fury of the flames, and women received back their dead, raised to life again. Faith and prayer are bedfellows. The above-mentioned recipients of the Hall of Fame were unrelenting prayer warriors in their field of the calling. David never embarked on any assignment without enquiring of the Lord. Moses was resilient in prayer that he was one of the few leaders who could plead with God to change his venomous acts against the people of Israel (Ex: 32: 9-14). Even Sampson at his death decimated so many philistines through prayer than the whole of his lifetime. Jesus conquered Satan on the cross by declaring the victory statement, "it is finished" John 19:30. Faith is the engine that propels prayer to effectual accomplishment.

## I was healed of ulcer

Over 20 years, I was an ulcer patient. In fact, my alimentary canal was in a bad condition and consequently an operation had to be performed on me to extract my appendix. Even though this was done, I still suffered so many traumas from duodenal ulcer. I had to go through my education with great difficulty but God being so good, he healed me at a communion service as well as from the word of God. Fellow theologians, I could not eat rice, beans and neither could I even take a sip of coffee. Now I am very free from the pain. The Lord has been so good and gracious to me. His love endures forever. Hallelujah!

Making prayer the unbroken habit and major force in your life will propel you into possessing spiritual fountain beyond your imagination. When you faint instead of praying, prayer becomes a farce instead of a magnetic force. When you cultivate the habit of studying the word of God couple with prayer you will soar like the eagle. The appropriate use of the word of God couple with ceaseless prayer, and being obedient to the word of God will definitely propel you into the presence of God, pleasing him and consequently, you will obtain a good report. Do you still have faith in God when circumstances are not favorable? When we have the kind of faith illustrated in Hebrews 11, we will please God, when we please Him, he will reward us, and when he rewards us, we will have good reports.

# CHAPTER 3

## PRAYER SOLVES MULTIPLE PROBLEMS

Sincere prayer moves the hand of God to solve diversity of problems confronting you, Isaiah chapters 36: 1-37; 37: 8-38 are two accounts of array of problems that the nation of Israel encountered during the reign of King Hezekiah. These scriptures highlight the Assyrian invasion, Rabshakeh's, threat, Assyrian fights, and Assyrian's threat. In the Assyrian attack, Rabshakeh, the King of Assyria tries to show the hopelessness of the resistance against Assyria. He points out the unrealistic support of Egypt and mocks Judah's ability to mount a serious military force.

The second Assyrian attack (37: 8-38) begins with a letter. The letter states **"Do not let the God you depend on deceive you when he says,** "Jerusalem will not be handed over to the King of Assyria.

Hezekiah responded to these threats with divine commands. He approached the problems from godly point of view. In Isaiah 37: 4-20, the King went to the Temple and spread the letter before the almighty God. He prays to Him. When a diversity of problems is confronting you, you have to spread the problems before the King of kings and the Lord of Lords. He is the Jehovah Shabaoth, the Lord of host, who fights our battles for us. Through his prayer, God promised to cut down Sennacherib, the King of Assyrian arrogance.

The next blessing that followed Hezekiah's prayer was that the nation of Israel would be able to resume the normal agricultural processes in the third year after the loss of two harvests caused by the Assyrian invasion.

The third blessing that came after his prayer was that God kept his promise of smiting the Assyrian army. He also stuck down Sennacherib. Hezekiah was the type of King who knew what to do in times of personal and national calamities. He took the matter to the King of Kings and the Lord of host. Certain facts such as the sovereignty of God; the incommunicable characteristics of God cannot be changed. God laid the universe from the beginning of creation. You cannot change God because God is spirit and they that worship him must worship in spirit and in truth (John 4: 24). You cannot change the fact that we have three persons in the Godhead: God the father, God the son, and God the Holy Spirit. You cannot change the fact that Jesus came in the flesh of man to die for the damnation of our sins. Nevertheless, we can change circumstances and seemingly impossible situations if we surrender our emotions, needs and desires to God. Just as Hezekiah overcame the most powerful military prowess of the Assyrians, so are we capable of conquering ungodly kingdoms and turning the tables in our favor. Take your needs to the right source, and you will be tremendously helped. When you take godly steps in addressing your problems, the Lord will usher you into experiencing undeniable breakthroughs to the amazement of your adversaries. Prayer directed to only the monotheistic God is the solution to a myriad of problems.

## HEZEKIAH HEALED OF SICKNESS (ISAIAH 38)

This text educates us to pray unceasingly. Hezekiah, even though received a death sentence from the Lord through the prophet Isaiah, he refused to give up. He prayed relentlessly to God. We still have to pray when dicey situations confronts us. **Prayer changes so many situations** .His sickness was placed during the time of Sennacherib's invasion. He became very sick to the point of death. Many think he fell sick because of the siege. Others explain that his sickness was because of a nervous breakdown in body and spirit, since it is certain that the king was subject to great anxiety in those days. The prophet Isaiah told him to set his house in order because he was going to die. It was shocking to him because he was only 39 years of age. The sentence of death was a terrible message for the King, who turned his face to the wall, wept, and prayed. Hezekiah pleaded for his dear life. The main reason for his weeping and prayer was the fact that he had no son to succeed him when if he died. Manasseh had not yet been born. Thus, the throne of Davidic kingdom was in jeopardy. He turned his face to the wall and wrestled with God. He prayed. He was a man of prayer. Whenever there was a kind of crisis in his life, he poured out his heart before the face of the Lord. He was not only an active ruler but also a praying King.

After presenting his credentials to God and pleading with Him, the answer to his prayer came very quickly. According to II Kings 20: 4, Isaiah was still in the palace when the word of the Lord came to Him requesting him to tell the king that God had heard his prayer. God heard his prayer and saw his tears because he had been so concerned with the house of David. Not only was he healed and his years elongated, the Holy city was not to fall into the hands of Sennacherib that also meant good health to Hezekiah.

The sickness of Hezekiah did not only traumatize him, it was also a major misfortune to the people of God. His death would mean that the Kingdom would fail to have an heir to succeed him since he had no son as at that time. Davidic throne was threatened of extinction. His prayer on the contrary was a perfect example for the people in the Kingdom to emulate since it did not only heal him but also made God to avert the siege by the King of Assyrians. . You can change certain things in your life. Hezekiah changed the land between two world powers of the time, Egypt and Assyria. He was 38 years old when he became King of Israel. He fell sick and was at the point of death. He also changed a premature death sentence into longevity of life. God in His mercies added 15 years to his life.

This implies that whenever we receive heart throbbing news, we should not grief over it, but rather we should turn to God in prayer. Even though Hezekiah was asked to organize his affairs because he was going to die, he did not throw in the towel. He sought the face of God with weeping and prayer. He was not just an active King but also a prayerful man. We need to pray all of the time for the intervention of God in similar situations. If he did not pray for longevity of life he would have died at age 39.

In conclusion, Abraham, Moses, Elijah, and Hezekiah prayed for God's intervention in specific situations in their lives. Abraham pleaded with God not to destroy Sodom and Gomorrah, Moses requested God in Exodus 32, not to wipe away the rebellious and stiff-necked people. In this scripture, we see a similar prayer offered by Hezekiah to relent his decision and save his life and the city of Jerusalem. This is a clarion call to all Christians to rise up and pray for the intervention of God in nations and Kingdoms. To rescue the perishing, make a way for the proclamation of the gospel, and for healing the sick, and the broken hearted.

## JONAH PRAYED IN THE BELLY OF A FISH

Jonah's gross dereliction of duty and the consequence of been swallowed up by a mighty whale cannot be glossed over. He shirked his divine responsibility of carrying the oracles of God to the city of Nineveh. In addition, in so doing he had to escape from the presence of God via a boat. He was thrown overboard when he and other sailors were engulfed in tumultuous waves and storms. Consequently, the mighty whale swallowed him up believing he had a sumptuous human meal. This meant that there was no route of escape whatsoever. Nevertheless, something spectacular took place. Prayer was the only antidote for survival. The Bible categorically asserts, "From inside the fish Jonah prayed to the Lord his God. He said, in my distress I called to the Lord, and he answered me. From the depths of the grave I called for help, and you listened to my cry"

(Jonah 2:1-2). His predicament in the belly of the fish was beyond life imprisonment. His perilous situation as well as his emotional, psychological and physical trauma could not be measured by any human endeavor. He was at the point of death. The **die** was cast, the Rubicon crossed, the verdict was pronounced, the executioners-fellow sailors had done their job, and the whale accomplished it by swallowing him up. Nevertheless, he did not throw in the towel. He used what was available to extricate his life from a dungeon of a fish belly. It was a dicey situation, which needed a rapid response via spiritual virtues and tools. He had to resort to prayer. The belly of the fish constituted a prison of death. He was out of his comfort zone. No oxygen, no friends, no loved ones, no pastors, no priests, and no neighbors. Yet he had to act all by himself to overcome such a calamitous circumstance of his life. Jonah reiterates, "When my life was ebbing away, I remembered you, Lord, and my prayer rose to you, to your holy Temple" (Jonah 2:7). When your life is ebbing away and you fail to hold the pieces together, remember the Lord in prayer.

When your business fails to yield the desired dividends, remember the Lord in prayer. When you fall sick or receive a bad report from your doctor, remember your God. You can only unlock your glorious destiny in the 21st century by praying. Jonah prayed in perilous situations and received divine answers. If you pray, your life will change around for the good and not for the worse. Furthermore, the Bible affirms in an intriguing statement, *"And the Lord commanded the fish and it vomited Jonah onto dry land" (Jonah 2:10).* Through relentless prayer in the belly of the fish, Jonah was vomited onto the dry land. Whatever seemed to have swallowed you up, when you pray, it would vomit you out. Whatever situation might have engulfed you, when you pray, you will be extricated form such a terrifying situation. Whatever seems to be irreversible situation in your life, when you pray it will be reversed. Whatever appears to be unsolvable, prayer is the antidote. Are you swallowed up by the Economic recession? Prayer will illuminate you and give you divine breakthroughs. Are you traumatized by divorce or disease? Prayer will help you survive the canker worms of our times. You are born to win. You are destined to be a champion. You are crafted to lead. You become a pacesetter when you pray. You realize your dreams and goals when you pray.

## Paul and Silas Prayed

In acts chapter 16, Paul and his counterpart, Silas used prayer to overcome a precarious and debilitating situation in their lives as they embarked on the second missionary journey. Through demon possession, a slave girl earned substantial amount of money for her owners. She predicted the future and engaged in fortune telling to amass wealth for her masters. She however followed Paul and Silas for several days proclaiming that they were servants of the most high. Paul became enraged and cast out the *pneumatikos* (evil spirits) out of her. She immediately became incapacitated in her career and could not make money through fortune telling. This aroused an uproar in the city, leading to the dragging of the Apostles to the magistrate who ordered them to be thrown into jail. They were stripped naked and severely flogged. They were subsequently thrown into jail, specifically in the inner cells where their feet were fastened to stocks. In the Roman empire, a jailor who was put in the inner cell meant that he was destined to be severely tortured. The fact that the two were put in the inner cell meant that beating, maltreatment, human right abuse continued in the jail. Their feet being fastened to the stocks meant that there was no route of escape. Stocks were crafted out of two boards joined together with iron clamps, creating holes wide enough for the ankles to be fitted in. The prisoner's legs were placed in the lower board, then the upper board would be placed across the lower board. There were times that both wrists were also placed in stocks.

In this case, Paul and Silas who had committed no crime and had propagated the Gospel of peace were put in stocks designated for the most dangerous, and notorious criminals. This in my view was psychologically sapping, mentally deflating and spiritually challenging. The verdict once again was pronounced and nothing in human endeavor could save them. The decision of the judge and the public was irreversible. Their trial in the kangaroo court, and denial of justice by the Roman government did not deter them. They had every excuse to fail as committed apostles and missionaries, and yet they were devoted to their calling as apostles to the Gentile nations. Despite all odds, Paul and Silas did something impressive. In the inner cell where there were no other believers, no other apostles, no an advocate or an attorney to plead on their behalf, they still performed undeniable miracles through Christomorphic prayers. The Bible declares, "About midnight, Paul and Silas were praying and singing hymns to God, and the other prisoners were listening to them" (Acts 16:25). Prayer was the **key** for their deliverance. They prayed and sang hymns. Before the New Testament was written, hymns were written using Jesus' name and his teachings. So singing hymns meant they directly called on Jesus for deliverance. Their Christocentric prayer made heaven to respond to their plight. Suddenly, there was an earthquake, the prison foundation was shaken, prison doors flung opened, and their chain broke loose. Prayer is a producer of undeniable miracles. They were delivered from the venom of the magistrate, the public and the Roman government.

In the 21st century, Christomorphic prayers will deliver you from prison of problems. Christocentric prayer will deliver you and bestow the justice of God on you. Paul and Silas were denied justice but justice was given when heaven responded via their prayer. Death sentences will be reversed if you employ Christocentric prayers. Life sentences will be reduced if you know your God and use his name in times of dicey situations. Financial imprisonment, possibly due to lack of managerial skills will be resolved through these types of prayers. The next aspect is that the Apostles prevented the jailer from committing suicide. Through fervent prayer, a true believer still saves lives in times of personal calamities. Physically, the jailer was saved from self-inflicting trauma and death. Spiritually, he received Christ as his Lord and savior. The third aspect is that through prayer, those who are saved by your committed missionary activities will take care of you. They will dress your wounds of life and feed you. You will not be forsaken, this is because the jailer took care of them and dressed up their wounds. The last point is that the jailer was saved from the venomous judgments of the magistrate and the Roman government. Your prayer saves millions and billions from death, from hunger, from financial woes and poverty. Renew your mind and channel your discussion to productive ventures. " **Great minds discuss ideas, average minds discuss events, small minds discuss people.**" By Hugh C. Cameron.

## KING ASA PRAYED

Second chronicles 14:9-14 is about the kingly rule of Asa of Judah. His reign was marked by peace because he did what was right in the eyes of God. He was a repairer of broken walls, and a builder of Ancient ruins. He was a town and territory developer. He believed in flamboyant and fortified structures. Based on his leadership dexterities, he constructed the fortified cities of Judah because of peace permeating every nook and cranny of the kingdom. He also undertook spiritual Reforms. Scripture explicates, "he removed the foreign altars and the high places, smashed the secret stones and cut down the Asherah poles. He removed the High places and incense altars in every town in Judah, and the kingdom was at peace under him" (2 Chr 14:2-6). He vehemently refused to worship foreign gods but rather engaged in ecclesiastical reforms bringing purity and monotheism to all the people of Judah.

For instance, Samuel exhorted the Israelites in I Sam. 7:3 to get rid of the foreign gods and the *Ashtoreths* in order to commit their lives to *Yahweh* alone. The Israelites obeyed and destroyed their *Baals* and *Ashtoreths* and served Yahweh only. Baal was believed to be the son of *El,* the supreme deity of the Canaanites. He was venerated and upheld as the god of thunder and rain, controlling vegetation and agriculture. *Ashtoreth* was the goddess of love and war. She was called *Ishtar* in Babylon and *Astante* or *Aphrodite* in

Greece. She was also upheld as the goddess of fertility. The Canaanites believed that coitus between Baal and Ashtoreth would magically rejuvenate the earth and make it more fertile and hospitable. These pagan influences made the Israelites to believe that they could resort to them for political, social, and national solutions. Samuel exhorted them to rid themselves of such undesirable and sacrilegious objects and anchor their faith in Yahweh only. Idolatry is making anything more significant in our lives than God-the creator of heavens and the earth. Actually, it is described as anything that wields power, and has the fervor to convert our hearts from God to adoring such a personality or object. It is a major source of temptation that plunges the soul and mind of the individual into deception, confusion, false security, and pretentious belief.

Furthermore, the surrounding nations sacrificed human beings to Baal. It was a gruesome practice where children were roasted in fire. They priests of Ball barbecued human flesh. On the contrary, king Asa destroyed the Baal god as well as the Asherah poles. Because of his deeds, God loved him and protected him. He refused to practice polytheism. He anchored his faith in God only. He also enjoined citizens of the southern kingdom of Judah to fear God and serve him only. Homogeneously, going to Church alone is not sufficient to please God. As 21st century believers, we are encouraged to remove anything that is god in our lives. For example, the god of a psyche must be removed. The gods of murder, lust, homosexuality, money laundry, voodoo consultation, robbery, embezzlement, slander, wickedness, stealing, adultery, fornication, anger, war, envy, jealousy, discrimination, conspiracy, witchcraft manipulation, sorcery, despise of one's neighbor, racism, tribalism, hatred of foreigners (xenophobic), ethnocentrism, juju for riches, and ancestral worship must be decimated. As a good king, he also undertook military enlistment and training. Scripture incisively declares, "Asa had an army of three hundred thousand men from Judah, equipped with large shields and with spears, and two hundred and eighty thousand from Benjamin, armed with small shields and with bows. All these were brave fighting men" (2 Chr 14:8). The only two tribes of the southern kingdom, Judah and Benjamin on this occasion formed a unified force in military prowess.

Furthermore, good leaders bring about prosperity. Asa declared, "Let us build up these towns, he said to Judah, put walls around them, with towers, gates and bars. The land is still ours, because we have sought the Lord, our God; we sought him and he has given us rest on every side. SO THEY BUILT AND ***PROSPERED***" (2chr 14:7). Unvaryingly, while the king was still consorting with the community of Yahweh people with the cardinal aim of extending development projects to other cities of Judah, a vast and heart-wrenching problem confronted him. Zerah the cushite marched out against them. Since the cushites attacked them, they had to fight the battle. Asa and his people went out and took up battle positions in the valley of Zephathah. Asa did not throw in the towel but called upon the name of his God. **"Then Asa called to the Lord his God and said, Lord there is no one like you to help the powerless against the mighty. Help us, Oh Lord, our God, for we rely on you, and in your name we have come against this vast army. O Lord, you are our God; do not let man prevail against you" (2 Chr 14:11).**

Prayer is the centrifugal force that is used to annihilate Satan's attacks as well as extricating oneself form the grip of problems. In this instance, king Asa resorted to theo-centric prayer to overcome life-threatening problems confronting the nation of Judah. The Bible explains that Asa's prayer brought unfathomable and heart-warming victory to the people of Yahweh. The Lord of Asah and Judah struck down the cushite army. The cushites were well trained charioteers who wielded military prowess and knew the terrain and battle tactics and strategies of their time, and yet prayer vanquished them. Scriptures declares, **"The Lord struck down the Cushites before Asa and Judah. The Cushites fled, and Asa and his army pursued them as far as Gerar. Such a great number of Cushites fell that they could not recover; they were crushed before the Lord and his forces. The men of Judah carried off a large amount of plunder. They destroyed all the villages around Gerar, for the terror of the Lord had fallen upon them. They plundered all these**

**villages, since there was much booty there. They also attacked the camps of the herdsmen and carried off droves of sheep and goats and camels. Then they returned to Jerusalem" (2 Chr 14:12-15).**

It is only those who employ the medium of prayer in the 21st century that will overcome perilous situations of their lives. Prayer provoked the assistance of Yahweh-Tsebbhaot, the God of the armies of Israel to fight the battle for them. Just as the Lord struck down the Cushites, prayer will invite God to annihilate every cushite-like problem in your life. Just as their villages and herdsmen were destroyed, anything that appears to be cushite-like attack will also be decimated. The battle ended in favor of the people of Judah. After that battle, their financial situation changed for the better. They carried large amount of plunder back to Jerusalem. So much booty was made available to them after their enemy was conquered. Every battle of life you overcome brings you promotion and financial blessings. They chalked success because they called on the right person. They also carried off droves of sheep, goats and camels. In the ancient near East, one mark of a prosperous household or community depended largely on the number of animals one possessed. Therefore, carrying off such magnitude of valuable domesticated animals increased their prosperity level. Prayer will lead to the defeat of your enemies, and the annihilation of your enemies will usher you into an arena of abundant prosperity. Ladies and Gentlemen, do not joke with prayer because what is going to bring you victory is by the word of your mouth in the domain of Christocentric and Elohistic centered prayers. If king Asa and his people had not prayed, their situation would have plunged the nation of Judah into appalling, and a deplorable state. The Cushites would have defeated them and might have made sausages out of them. Nevertheless, their prayer gave them a U-Turrn of victory. Victory over the attacking enemy brought them unfathomable wealth.

Another aspect of their victory was that prayer brought about the terror of the Lord upon the Cushites. Until you pray to the omnipotent God, the enemy of life and progress remains fearless. Prayer undoubtedly brings terror upon every foe that rises up against you. Because the Cushites were terrified, defeating them was so easy. An enemy who is afraid is easily conquered.

Rehab, a prostitute of Jericho recounted to the spies the fear and trepidation effects of the Exodus narrative on her kith and kin. Hence, made the following confession, "When we heard of it, our hearts melted and everyone's courage failed because of you, for the LORD your God is God in heaven above and on the earth below (Josh 2:11). When the people of Jericho heard the miraculous work of God in delivering the Israelites from severe bondage in Egypt, and their miraculous escape at the Red sea, their hearts melted. When your enemy is discouraged, traumatized and thrown into confusion, defeating him is so easy. The Israelites possessed Jericho, leading to the fall of the wall because the terror of God had fallen upon the inhabitants of Jericho. Trumpeting cum prayer as well as unsurpassable leadership skills brought down the wall of Jericho as terror gripped the heart of every person living in that city. Where God pours out his venom of terror on the enemy, defeating the enemy is so easy and prosperity and possession of the Land becomes your portion. King Asa and the nation of Judah in this instance annihilated the Cushites through prayer that brought untold terror upon them.

# CHAPTER 4

## PRAYER INVOLVES SPIRITUAL WARFARE

One of the most important themes unraveled to Christians of all generations in the book of Ephesians is the instruction on spiritual warfare. The author, Paul has spent a considerable amount of time deliberating on the need for believers to be aware of the spiritual battles that confront them every passing minute. It is in view of this that when writing to believers in the church of Ephesus he lays emphasis on our struggles, battles, challenges, conflicts in this present world. He asserts that our contention is not provoked against fellow human beings but unrelenting battle against supernatural beings. Believers are encouraged to adorn the spiritual armor that will afford them the opportunity to vanquish the enemy in the ensuing battle. The enemy, Satan, and his cohorts are on twenty-four hour duty every day deceiving and trying to deceive believers to forsake the path of righteousness. In order to maintain the victory that Christ won for us on the cross of Calvary we must make a concerted effort in putting on the full armor of God prescribed for all believers in Ephesians chapter 6: 10- 17.

## The Believer, and Spiritual Warfare (Ephesians 6: 10-17)

One of the most important themes unraveled to Christians of all generations in the book of Ephesians is the instruction on spiritual warfare in the kingdom of God. The kingdom of God is not just an arena of joy, peace, and tranquility. It also involves the fiercest conflict that confronts believers in every passing minute of their lives. The author, Paul has spent a considerable amount of time deliberating on the need for believers to be aware of the spiritual battles that confront them as they sojourn in the kingdom of God. When writing to believers in the Church of Ephesus he lays emphasis on our struggles, battles, challenges, and conflicts in this present world. He asserts that our contention is not provoked against fellow human beings but unrelenting battle against supernatural beings. Believers are encouraged to adorn the spiritual armor that will fortify them to vanquish the enemy in the ensuing battle. The enemy, Satan, and his cohorts are on twenty-four hour duty every day deceiving and trying to deceive believers to forsake the path of righteousness. In order to maintain the victory that Christ won for us on the cross of Calvary we must make a concerted effort in putting on the full armor of God prescribed for all believers in Ephesians chapter 6: 10- 17. Biblical scholars have proven beyond every shade of doubt that life was more a daunting task for the ancient Christians than the contemporary believers. According to William Barclay life was much more terrifying for the ancient people than it is for today. They believed implicitly in evil spirits, who filled the air and were determined to work men harm.[31] Similarly, Maxie D. Dunnam states that Demons, devils, and evil spirits haunted every corner of the ancient world. The whole universe was a battleground.[32]. Paul having been informed of these Greek mythologies and demons he challenges

---

[31] William Barclay, *The letters to the Galatians and the Ephesians* (Philadelphia: Westminster Press,1976), 182.

[32] Maxie D. Dunnam, *The communicator's Commentary: World Books* (Texas: WACO, 1982), 239.

all believers to put on the full armor of God. But first and foremost, they must be strong in the Lord and in the power of His might.

## BE STRONG IN THE LORD, AND IN THE POWER OF HIS MIGHT AND PUTTING ON THE FULL ARMOR OF GOD THAT YOU MAY BE ABLE TO STAND AGAINST THE WILES OF THE DEVIL (EPH. 6:10-11)

The apostle entreats his audience to be strong in the Lord and in the power of his might. Paul is exhorting them to find their strength in the Lord. They need to constantly draw upon the power they already possess through their union with Christ. To be strong in the Lord is further explained by the phrase, "and in the power of his might." Power denotes an active force, whereas might denotes a passive force, inherently possessed whether exercised or not. To be strong in the Lord denotes that the believer needs to be made aware that the battle is for the Lord himself who has already dealt a deadly blow to the forces of evil.[33]. The things that are commanded are impossible to perform without God's strength and grace. We need his strength and power to overcome our enemies, our flesh, and Satan. We need his strength to adorn the doctrine of Christ with holiness and integrity. Even though we are weak and can do nothing of ourselves, his grace is sufficient for all things.[34]The call "to be strong" in the face of a severe battle is prototype of Old Testament scriptures, the most obvious refers to Joshua, who was commanded "to be strong and of good courage" (Joshua 1: 6-7, 9). Correspondingly, David also found strength in the Lord when the Amalekites invaded Ziklag (1 Sam

---

[33] Willard .H Taylor. *Beacon Bible expositions: Galatians and Ephesians* (Kansas City: Beacon Hill Press, 1982), 209.
[34] Henry T. Maham. *Bible class Commentary* (England: Evangelical Press, 1991), 68.

82

30:6). When the remnants returned from the Babylonian captivity, God declared, "I will make them strong in the Lord (Zech. 10:12).[35]

The verse 11 gives a picture of a Soldier standing firm in battle. Paul having been arrested a number of times by Roman soldiers and having also witnessed the soldiers in combating positions is fully aware of the dress code of the Roman combatant in his era. The believer lives in the world of evil. Evil powers and evil people surround him. The believer also has his armor and therefore Paul takes the Roman soldier and contextualizes him into Christian terms. This world is not the friend of grace or God. Not only is sin around us, but also sin is within us. The Christian life is a race to be run (Heb. 6:12; 2Tim 4:7). We need strength and help to stand up against all of the deceit and strategies of Satan, who is the greatest enemy of Christ and his people. God has provided armor for his people and weapons to be used against Satan, sin, and error.[36].

## WE DO NOT WRESTLE AGAINST FLESH AND BLOOD, THEREFORE TAKE UP THE FULL ARMOR OF GOD (EPH. 6:12-13)

This verse portrays that we are not contending against physical opponents. Frail, moral men are not our enemies. Our battle is against wicked spirits, who inhabit the supernatural sphere and who deal in lies, pride, idolatry, covetousness, lust, deceit, self-righteousness, and all manner of sin against God. The Greek word for wrestle is *pale* meaning "to struggle", "to fight", and "to combat." The forces threatening Christians as they live out their lives in Christ

---

[35] Peter T. Obrian, *The Letter to the Ephesians* (Grand Rapids, Michigan: William B. Eerdmans, 1999), 461. Peter T. obrian further elucidates that the apostle might have been thinking of Is. 40:26 as he wrote Eph. 6:10 since the terms *kratos and lochuos* are related to this Old Testament passage, and hence the author is indebted to Isaiah for his terms and metaphors.

[36] Henry T. Maham. *Bible class Commentary* (England: Evangelical Press, 1991), 69.

are not only those, which arise out of human context, but also those emanating from the supernatural evil order. Human ingenuity and strength are woefully in adequate to withstand the advancement of these powers of evil.[37] Thus, the Bible aptly describes the opponent as spirit beings and not flesh and blood, (pros *aima kais ark*). "In heavenly places" suggest the realm of spiritual conflict. No matter how spiritually stable, reverential, and prayerful God's people might be, they are never immune from the attack by the wicked spiritual forces.[38]

The spiritual battle is *pros tas archas* "against the principalities, and *pros tas exousiai* "against the powers." This designates the demons according to the powers or ranks which resonate with the classes of angels where principalities are classified in the higher rank than the *exousiai* "powers."[39] The next clause states, *pros tous epouraviois* "against the World rulers in heavenly places" is a condensed explanation of the World expanse and its ethical quality. The world rulers are superhuman, and they are super-terrestrial enemies. Strikingly, principalities, the powers, and the rulers of the world belong to this "darkness." The World rulers refer to *kosmoskrator,* connoting the world-ruling gods.[40] They are spirit beings that have part of the *kosmos* "world" under their control. They wield territorial dominance in some part of the *kosmos*. In rabbinic writing, these spirits are referred. to as angels of death. That is the *kosmos* "world", and people who are not born again are subject to them. Semanticists believe that the **World tyrants** is better a term than the **World rulers.**[41] Accordingly, the devils are called *kosmoskratores* because their dominion is felt everywhere in the world except the kingdom of God where Jesus is the supreme commander, and sovereign Lord over the universe. The clause, "The

---

[37] Peter T. Obrian, *The Letter to the Ephesians* (Grand Rapids, Michigan: William B. Eerdmans, 1999), 463.

[38] Ibid., 463.

[39] Ibid., 463.

[40] Ibid., 463.

[41] Ibid., 463-464.

spiritual hosts of wickedness in the heavenly places" describes all the powers of evil vigorously working in the unseen hierarchical order under the auspices of the archenemy, Satan. A spiritual host in Greek is *pneumatikos*, pertaining to evil spirits, or "the forces of evil." Theses spirits are not friendly or sympathetic; they exhibit *ponerias* "wickedness" towards humankind, especially believers who are called to live above reproach.[42] The word implies "wickedness", "baseness", "maliciousness", "viciousness", "spitefulness", "ferociousness", and "sinfulness."

If Satan stood valiantly against Jesus after he fasted forty days and forty nights, employing all sorts of diabolical maneuvers to lure Jesus into gross disobedience to his Father, then nobody is immune from his venomous attacks. He tried to ensnare Jesus with food (Mt. 4:3-4). He also took Jesus to the Temple top and tried to deceive him to test God in disobedience (Mt. 4-7). He also led Jesus to the mountaintop and requested him to worship him (Mt. 4: 8-11). Satan is a defeated foe. We only need to lace up our boots of morality and beef up our spiritual forces to ward him off our domain. Having been exposed to the realities of spiritual warfare, Paul therefore exhorts his readers to be prepared by wearing **"the whole armor of God."** It is very clear that the armor of God provided is adequate for the battle. To withstand implies, "a stand against great opposition." It is imperative for the Christian to adequately prepare for both active and passive style of defense to secure a safety. The Christian soldier must be active, and passive in raising, attacking, defending oneself from the malicious attack of the enemy. The Greek word for "take up" is *amalambon,* meaning the Christian warrior must take up the armor of God always as we sojourn in the kingdom of God.[43] It is an imperative, demanding all regenerated believers to obey. Refusal to take the armor of God would result in dire consequences of trauma, defeat, sicknesses, impediment to the proclamation of the Gospel of peace, and absolute lack of peace and victories. "The whole armor" translates the Greek word **panoplia** that can either

---

[42] Ibid., 463-464.
[43] Ibid., 464-465.

mean "splendid **armor**" or **"complete armor."** Some scholars suggest a public display of the qualities of truth, righteousness, peace, and faith.[44] Nevertheless, some suggest that the element of completeness seems more appropriate since Paul is concerned in this passage to call Christians to depend upon God's power for victory over wickedness. The armor has no protection for the back. The expectation of Paul is that the Christian has no defense anyhow if he retreats from trusting the Lord. The evil Day may be taken to mean " **the present age"** or the particular day when the military powers of "the heavenly places" attack, which even though vanquished by Christ still wield power to exercise over a world that does not avail itself of the fruits of Christ's victory.[45] Since Satan is involved in surface-to-surface spiritual missile attack against Christians, believers need a missile defense system that will protect and equip them to assault the enemy and defend themselves from his aggressive attacks. The only way to achieve this is to don the full armor of God. Like the soldier or the marine, the Christian is commanded to be combat-ready at all times. Therefore, the expression, "to withstand" *anthistemi* in Greek signifies "setting oneself against, oppose, and resist."[46] So taking up the full armor of God will prepare the believer in the kingdom to successfully resist the enemy. The opposition is great and ferocious, and the conflict is imminent. It is only when believers take up the full armor of God that they can "stand their ground." That is they must fiercely resist the adversary, stand up against him, and totally repulse him.

The evil day on the contrary connotes worsening of situations and circumstances. When the enemy attacks and things seem to get out of control leading to the worst of all situations then there is appearance of the evil day. Actually, the evil day is a day of trial. It is the day that enemies will make their assault. Nevertheless, this is

---

[44]  Ibid., 164.

[45]  Willard .H Taylor. *Beacon Bible expositions, Galatians and Ephesians,* (Kansas City: Beacon Hill Press, 1982), 210.

[46]  William Barclay, *The letters to the Galatians and the Ephesians,* (Westminster Press 1976),183.

not the eschatological conflict before the Second Advent. The attack of *poneros* (the evil one) is pre-imminent, and moral evil is combat-ready to launch the fiercest attack against believers. After having *ketargazomai* "achieved, accomplished, overpowered, subdued, and conquered", and after proving victorious over every daunting problem, then the believer must stand his ground against the virulent attacks of the archenemy and his cohorts. Paul dilates on a desperate combat in which the soldier exhibits excellence in the performance of his duties, and still strives on when his cause seems to be doomed to failure. The Christian similarly is to stay strong in battle, when he runs outs of energy.

## GIRDING THE WAIST WITH TRUTH, PUTTING ON THE BREASTPLATE OF RIGHTEOUSNESS, AND PROCLAIMING THE GOSPEL OF PEACE (EPH. 6: 14-15)

Scholars have proven that the girdle was a belt and it's most immediate and practical use for a soldier was to gird or hold his tunic so that he could move about freely without any obstruction. Alternatively, the girdle was worn around the loins roviding a frame for free, and vigorous action. The idea is that the girdle was the bracer up, or supporter of the body, therefore truth is fitted to brace up and to gird us for constancy and firmness. It also provided an abode to hang his sword. The imagery here is that truth holds together all other virtues and makes them effectual. The belt was not mere adornment of the soldier, but it adequately prepared the soldier to fashion out the Amory appropriately. Even though the girdle was not part of the armor, it was required to be properly fitted before the armor could be adorned. It was highly ornamented and served as a saved haven for transportation of money, the sword, the pipe, and stationary. Truth is to be understood here not as the gospel in the objective sense but the gospel as been lived by faith. The Christian soldier lives in truth, faithfulness, loyalty, and sincerity. Righteousness refers to the right conduct or practice. In Isaiah 59: 17, the prophet pictures God as putting on "righteousness as a breastplate and a helmet of salvation upon his head." The breastplate of *dikaiosune* (righteousness) suggests the protecting quality of holiness. William Barclay writes that when a man is clothed in righteousness he is impregnable.[47] Righteousness energizes the believer's heart and renders it inaccessible to the hostile activities of the devil and demons. For the believer to vanquish the whims and caprices of the enemy, holiness is required. Satan fears holiness and crumbles in the face of a holy Christian. The clause, *perizonnumi* (having girded), implies, "gird about, and gird oneself".[48]

Moreover, Sandals in the ancient times were the sign of one equipped and ready to move. The sandals were to preserve the foot from danger and to shelter the capability of his march, most probably to make the combatant dauntless in battle. It has been said that the attention given to the soldiers' boots was the secret of the Roman conquest.[49] Christians are enjoined to have the principles and discipline of the Gospel peace so that they can remain valiant in the day of battle with the adversaries. The shoe in Paul's opinion is to allow the Christian soldier move with agility, briskly, and fight gallantly against the enemy.[50] The Greek word is *hetoimaisia*, which implies "readiness, preparation" for *euaggelion tes eirenes*, "the Gospel of peace." The sign of a Christian is that he is ever ready and eager to undertake a journey of righteousness to share the word of God with others who have not heard it.[51] It is a known fact that the military boots, stood out as one of the most significant aspects of the armory of the Roman soldier's equipment. They were designed

---

[47] Ibid., 183.

[48] Ibid., 211.

[49] Maxie D. Dunnam, *The Comentator's Commentary: Word Books*, (Texas:WACO, 1982), 241.

[50] William Barclay, *The letters to the Galatians and the Ephesians*, (Westminster Press 1976), 182.

[51] Maxie D. Dunnam, *The Comentator's Commentary: Word Books*, (Texas:WACO, 1982), 242-243.

for long marches over both smooth and rugged terrains. I repeat, "It has been said that the attention given to the soldiers' boots was the secret of the Roman conquest." The believer may encounter a number of difficulties in spreading the gospel but the gospel lays a solid foundation in our faith in Christ. The Christian soldier must possess a dauntless missionary zeal, a call that signals the preparedness, or readiness to proclaim the Gospel of peace everywhere. Since according to the prophets, peace was to form an essential part of the messianic hope and kingdom, Christian ideology fathoms *eirene* "peace" as synonymous with messianic salvation.

## THE SHIELD OF FAITH AND THE HELMET OF SALVATION (EPH. 6:16-17)

In ancient warfare, the soldier or marine had a problematical task of defending himself against every missile that his foes threw at him. The shield was a double-ply, oblong wooden shield worn by the heavily armed combatant. It covered the entirety of his body, measuring two and half by four feet, and curved on the inside. It protected the warrior from the most dangerous of all ancient weapons, the fiery dart.[52] Therefore, the shield was designed to stop the dart and extinguish the flame. Thus, marines and soldiers seriously regarded it as one of the perilous weapons used in battle. The heads of the darts or arrows were covered with flax or hemp fiber, soaked in pitch, and then set on fire before they were thrown. It was so easy for wooden shields to be set ablaze. To prevent the shields from burning they were covered with hide and were long enough to protect the whole body. The Greek word, *sbennumi* meaning, "to quench", "extinguish", and "put out something" symbolically, fiery darts is apt for explanation. Whenever the fiery darts collided with the shields, their points blunted, and their flames extinguished leaving the soldier unharmed. Since burning arrows had double potency of piercing and setting the soldiers on flames, they were

---

[52] Ibid.,242-243.

89

metaphorically considered as the fiercest weaponry used by Satan. He constantly throws missile in the form of fiery darts against the soul of the believer; who if unprotected by the shield of faith would soon perish. It is common experience of believers that at times undesirable thoughts, lack of faith, unholy attitude toward the word of God, blasphemous utterances and activities, skepticism, and malignant thoughts crowd the mind and souls of the believer, which cannot easily be disentangled. These are often allusions to the relentless attacks by Satan, which if not checked will plunge the believer in a very precarious situation. Faith in this regard is a shield protecting the believer against both visible and invisible attacks.

Furthermore, Paul has a longing for Isaiah who sees God as "a helmet of salvation upon his head" (59:17). The Greek word for helmet is *perikephalalia* and sword is translated as *machairan*. Hence when the Christian soldier has taken his stand, well-girt with breastplate, shoes, shield, he still needs helmet and sword to accomplish his military task in the kingdom. Just as the soldier receives the helmet and sword from the armor-bearer, the Christian soldier *amalabete* (takes, receives) his gifts from the Lord. The helmet in itself is salvation, thus salvation, *soterios* is of messianic "salvation" and Christ is the one who mediates it. The helmet guides the center of life. The sense and hope of salvation transcends life beyond the comprehensibility of human imagination because it protects the combatant from assaults of the evil one aimed at his zeal and righteousness in the kingdom of God. As the helmet defends the head from the fiery punches of the devil, a well-founded hope of salvation preserves, protects and gives us victory over the enemy on the day of conflict. Maxie educates that the helmet does not provide protection for the carrier, but is a symbol of God's power and readiness to save others. Paul pictures this helmet of salvation put on by the Christian soldier, as the guarantee of divine protection and ultimate deliverance. He declares that salvation is not only forgiveness of past sins, it is strength to overcome, even conquer, present and future sins.[53]

---

[53] Ibid., 212.

In addition, the word of the spirit is aptly described as the word of God and that word "is quick and powerful, and sharper than any two-edged sword" (Heb. 4:12). Willard declares that the sword is the property of the spirit, and is the written word of God, the Holy Scriptures. It is the spirit who inspired the word of God and who now interprets the word to believers. All the other weapons are meant for defense but the sword of the spirit is a defensive weapon. Wesley comments, "We are to attack Satan, as well as secure ourselves; the shield in one hand, and the sword in the other. Whoever fights with the power of hell will need both."[54] Paul is exhorting all believers to put on the whole armor of God in order to overcome the enemy in our warfare with him. We should be able to vanquish sin, flesh, and the wiles of the enemy by finding our strength in the word of God and depending totally on him.

---

[54] Willard .H Taylor. *Beacon Bible expositions, Galatians and Ephesians,* (Kansas City: Beacon Hill Press, 1982), 212.

# CHAPTER 5

## TITHE AND OFFERING INTELLIGENCE.

Right investment, right expenditure, and right business contacts and undertakings will make you a prosperous personality. You really cannot produce wealth until you know how to invest the little income that you have. Every millionaire or a rich person employs the dexterity of business investment.)

A very important path to prosperity is **tithe payment.** You prosper by paying your tithe. You create wealth by giving offering. Thus, payment of tithe pleases God, when God is pleased; he flings open the doors and windows of prosperity. Tithe payment fortifies you against Satan. God rebukes Satan and his cohorts on your behalf. If you do not have Christocentric, logos, davar, or elohistic **intelligence,** you may not have the **intelligence of giving.** The intelligence of payment of tithe and offering emanates from one's divine connection. Abraham had elohistic intelligence, **he believed the Lord, and he credited it to him as righteousness (Gen. 15:6).** Noah had elohistic intelligence because he **"was a righteous man, blameless among the people of his time and he walked with God"** (Gen. 6:9). Enoch had elohistic **intelligence** because he walked with God. Jesus, the apostles and his disciples had Christocentric as well as Elohistic intelligence. In addition, because of immeasurable proportions of Elohistic and Christocentric intelligence they had, they collected offerings for the poor in the churches. Moreover, because Abraham was imbued with unchallenged magnitude of Elohistic intelligence, he paid tithe to Mechilzedeck. Hence, the dexterity to pay tithe, give offering, and do kindness to the poor emanates from the heart of the giver, which most of the time is connected to Elohim and Jesus Christ. Therefore, Malachi 3:8 declares, *"Will a man rob God? Yet you rob me. But you ask, how do we rob you? In tithes and offering. You are under a curse-the whole nation of you-because you are robbing me. Bring the whole tithe into the storehouse that there may be food in my house. Test me in this, says the Lord almighty, and see I will not throw open the floodgates of heaven and poor out so much blessing that you will not have room enough for it."*

When you pay tithe and offering, the Lord propels you into achieving greater things. When you pay your tithe and offerings, the Lord fights your financial battles for you. The **storehouse** refers to the treasury rooms of the sanctuary. It was a place where sacred articles and food were stored. The food was meant for the Levies, who administered before God. No Levite was to go hungry or without food except when they were fasting. The Levites did not till the land because God chose them to administer before him all the days of their lives. Therefore, the food in the storehouse was for them to enjoy and to set some apart for offerings. King Solomon placed the silver and the gold in the treasuries of the Lord's Temple (1Kings 7:51). Furthermore, **a floodgate is** a figurative term meaning the source of abundant blessing. It implies abundant supply of food, blessings, and unfathomable prosperity (2Kings 7:2, 19). It also connotes pouring out blessings or the promised covenant of God on his people. Thus, *"The Lord will open the heavens, the storehouse of his bounty, to send rain on your land in season to bless all the works of your hands. You will lend to many nations but will borrow from none"* (Deut. 28:12).

Scripture also declares, **"I give to the Levites all the tithe in Israel as their inheritance in return for the work they do while serving at the tent of meeting" (Num 18:21).** The tithes were meant for the Levites who led the congregation in worship of the Lord. They were not to be deprived of food, and daily living. Because God is honored when people congregate in his name, worshipping him in songs and in prayer, led by a sanctified priest or a pastor. There was cultic dereliction during the time of prophet Malachi. The people had forsaken the Lord, and had blatantly disobeyed God in the arena of tithing and offering. God warned them to turn from apostasy and serve him. Refusal to pay tithe and offering provoked unrelenting curse on the people of Yahweh. Do not get your finances cursed because you refuse to pay your tithes and offerings. On the contrary, if you obey the Lord in tithing and offering your barns will overflow, and your financial vats will brim with new wine. The Hebrew word for "happy", or "blessed" is *oshrii*[55]. This word has occurred 26 times in the Psalms, a classic example is Psalm 1: 1, which states, "Blessed is the man who does not walk in thc counsel of the wicked" The term" blessed is the man" is translated as *oshrii haish*. It carries the nuance of positivity in most places in the Book of Psalms[56]. Hence, the Lord will **bless the work of your hands** in Deut 28: 12 carries the connotation of high-level productivity in your endeavors. In your business, you are destined to be a person of unsurpassable productivity. At your job, in Church and in your family, your productivity level must exceed mediocrity and inferiority complex.

Leviticus 27:30 asserts, **"A tithe of everything from the land, whether grain from the soil, or fruits from the soil or fruits from the trees belong to the Lord. It is holy to the Lord."** Anything that is Holy to God comes with unsearchable blessings. If your tithe and offering are holy, they bring you unfathomable blessing. Thus, tithing prevents you from being selfish or greedy while at the same time expanding your financial territories. Tithing is a watershed or a focal point of blessing. **"Good will come to him who is generous"**

---

[55] Miles Van Pelt and Pratico D. Gary: *The Vocabulary Guide to Biblical Hebrew* (Grand Rapids, Michigan: Zondervan, 2003), 36.

[56] H.P Ruger A. Alt, O. Eibfeldt, P. Kahle ediderant, and R. Kittel eds, *Biblia Hebraica Stuttgartensia*: Stuttgarttensia, Vierte verbesserte Auflage, 1990], 1087. The following scriptures of the Book of Psalms that dilate on the word "ashree" are Psalms 41:1; 84:5; 106:3; 112:1; and 119:1.

(Pr. 112:5). "A generous man will prosper" (Pr. 11: 25). "A generous man will himself be blessed" (Pr. 22: 9).

## RIGHTEOUSNESS INTELLIGENCE

New Testament intellectuals have unanimously agreed that righteousness and the Kingdom are the two most significant themes of the Sermon on the Mount. They postulate that God conveys righteousness to his people as deliverance, and Christians studiously participate in it by executing righteous deeds. The Greek lexical item employed here is *dikaiosune*, and its root is *dike* having the overtone of justice. Jesus in this verse is succinctly quoting from (Isaiah 61:3, 10, 11) authenticating the administration of righteousness or justice. The Hebrew word is *tsedaqah*, which carries the nuance of administering justice that rescues and delivers the oppressed. *Tsedaqah* restores the immobilized and the rejected to their equitable place in covenant society. The word *tsedaqah* is equivalent to other words such as *mishpat* (Psalm 37). That is the cardinal reason why the hungry and the thirsty hunger and thirst for righteousness.[57]

Righteousness in the Old Testament implies fostering and conserving of peace in the community of God's people, and is sometimes used interchangeably with shalom, peace (Isaiah 32:16-17). The *tsedaqah* "justice", "righteousness" in Yahweh is fathomed in the deliverance of his people from the shackles of slavery in Egypt and ushering them into becoming covenant inhabitants of the Promised Land. There is copious evidence that Israel continued to appeal Yahweh's righteousness from deliverance, and from trouble (Pss31: 1; 143:11); from enemies (Pss 5:8í 143:1), from the wicked (Ps 36; 71:2), for vindication of her cause before her enemies (Ps 35:24), and Yahweh maintains the cause of the afflicted and needy (Ps 140: 12).

Additionally, Psalm 92: 12-15 states, ***"The righteous will flourish***

---

[57] Glen H. Stassen & David P. Gushee, *Kingdom Ethics* (Downers Grove, Illinois: Intervarsity Press, 2003), 41.

*like a palm tree, they will grow like the cedar of Lebanon; planted in the house of the* LORD, they *will flourish in the courts of our God. They will still bear fruit in old age, they stay fresh and green, "proclaiming, "The Lord is upright; he is my rock, and there is no wickedness in him."* The word **FLOURISH** means to grow luxuriantly, to prosper, to thrive, and to achieve success. It also means to be in the state of activity and productivity. Other words associated with **Flourish** are **grow, increase, burgeon, bourgeon blossom, boom, be successful, to do well, proliferate, multiple, to be prosperous or affluent.** Do you desire to flourish in in your business? Then be righteous. It is a biblical injunction that engenders prosperity and wealth. Righteous **intelligence is embedded in the word of God.** If you refuse to be righteous, and to undertake righteous activity, then prosperity will elude you. Businesses, established cooperate offices, Churches, theological, Biblical and ecclesiastical institutions will want to do business with a person who does things right. You must be right in your deeds. You must be right in your lifestyle. You must be right in executive, board, and leadership meetings. You cannot swim in the quagmire of mediocrity and expect to flourish. Businesses, and people who wield financial power as well as leadership dexterity are looking out for people who are right in their mental aptitude, right in their speech, right in their actions, right in their promises, right in their family affairs, and right in their undertaking. Until you possess **righteousness intelligence,** you will walk on gold in poverty. Palm trees are known for their long life. Thus, to flourish like the palm tree means to stand tall and to live long. When you are righteous, you always stand tall among your peers. You are always primus inteparis, a Latin term meaning first among equals. Stand tall in your business, in your leadership, in your family, in your neighborhood, and at your job. Do not allow people to despise, and emit out contemptible words against you. When you have **righteous intelligence**, people will be compelled to respect you and to honor you, and God.

Homogeneously, the cedars of Lebanon grew 120 feet in height and grew up to 30 feet in circumference; thus, they were solid, strong, and immovable. The righteous person is strong, determined, resolute, resilient, and unmoved by the winds of circumstances. If you are righteous by putting your faith in God, you will always bask in the invincible strength and vitality of the creator of heaven and the earth. Nevertheless, because we live in a corrupt world, with its corruptible nature, most people have the erroneous impression that lying, cheating, embezzlement, corruption, and unrighteous lifestyle, sexual promiscuity and fighting, killings and insults are the saviors that extricate them from poverty and problems. These factors are not bringing you financial emancipation; they will rather generate judgment and pour the venom of God's wrath upon you. These corruptible behaviors of human species will stimulate depression, famine, disgrace, disasters, and underperformance in human society. They are fortified to inoculate acrimony, pandemonium, disunity, poverty, lack of ingenuity, and lack of foresight into your endeavors.

The expression, **"They will flourish in the courts of our God"** is worthy of explanation. The courts of the Lord were a wide arena that worshippers congregated just before the entrance of the Temple or the worship edifice. It is postulated that anyone who entered the courts of the Lord with the intension of worshipping God was a candidate for abundant prosperity. Worshippers who gathered worshipped the Lord and so whatever was accredited to them, as blessing was part of those worshippers. If you want to prosper, the right place for unfathomable financial breakthrough and abundant wealth creation is the house of God. Worship God in the house of God. Praise him in his sanctuary, uplift his name in midst of other worshippers. By so doing the Lord will give you business ideas, he will connect you to the right people, he will make you succeed, because in Jesus our foundation is solid. Are you a child of God, paying tithe, giving offering, devotion to your God is not in vain. You are destined to prosper. You are ordained to hit financial headlines. You will not go unnoticed in your endeavors. The Lord will promote you. He would establish you like the cedar of Lebanon.

In Jesus' days, businesspersons corrupted the Temple courts. Instead of Worshipping God, they turned the temple into a stock exchange where magnitude proportions of profits were made. They did not only turn the temple courts into stock exchange market, but they also created forex bureaus where the worshippers were robbed off their monies through fraudulent means **"In the temple courts he found men selling cattle, sheep, and doves, and others sitting at tables exchanging money" (John 2:14).** The temple was overcrowded during the Jewish festival of Passover. Visitors from other towns thronged the Temple in Jerusalem. They temple leaders allowed merchants and moneychangers to set up booths in the gentile courts crowding out worshippers. In order for foreigners to pay their temple tax in full in local currency, they had to exchange their own currency for that of Jerusalem. Merchants took advantage of the situation and made massive proportions of money from the temple courts. Because of long distances, foreigners bought sacrificial animals from corruptible merchants, and by so doing, they paid exorbitantly for the animals. Jesus was enraged at the dishonest, and egocentric behavior of the moneychangers and merchants that he fashioned out a whip and lashed them.

The statement that, *"They will still bear fruit in old age, they stay fresh and green, "proclaiming, "The Lord is upright; he is my rock, and there is no wickedness in him"*, connotes high-level productivity in your old age. Even though you may be advanced in years, your productivity level soars like that of the eagle. Even though your business may be buffeted by winds of recession, you will still earn abnormal profits. Righteousness engenders the favor of God, prosperity, wealth creation, and the peace of God.

In addition, David declares in Psalm 52: 8 *"But I am like the olive tree flourishing in the house of God; I trust in God's unfailing love forever and ever."* David compared himself to the olive tree flourishing in the house of God. *It is metaphorical idiom, like the Lord is my shepherd, or I am the light of the world, or I am the bread of life.* A metaphor is a figure of speech whose meaning is embedded in the statement, and must be unraveled before its denotation or its tacit connotation is comprehended. Praying in the house of God is a righteous deed. Giving offering and paying tithe in the house of God is a righteous deed. Showing compassion and love for the poor and the needy is a righteous deed. What is the significance of an olive tree? The olive tree is one of the longest living trees in human history or in the world's vegetative cover. It has the ability to flourish in both favorable and unfavorable circumstances. In the forest belt of the near East, the olive tree had greater longevity than most trees. The righteous person must flourish like the olive tree in his or her endeavors. The righteous has access to longevity of life. If you are not flourishing, find out whether you have **righteousness intelligence.** True to the word of King David, he was so old that they had to look for a beautiful Midianite woman to administer to him. He was fed, bathed, clothed and encouraged by a young beautiful woman in his old age. In righteousness, you do not die young. I was watching TBN a few days ago, when I saw a parade of men of God wishing Billy Graham a happy 94[58] birthday. Those who wished him a happy birthday were Pastor John Hagee of Cornerstone Church in Texas, Bishop TD Jakes of the Porter's House, Texas, Pastor parsley of Columbus, Ohio, Dr. Lloyd Olgivie, Two governors, many other men of God and TBN family. As a man who wielded **righteousness intelligence** all his years, he had access to divine longevity. He is a classic living example of a righteous man living like **an olive tree.** He spent his entire life evangelizing the world, delivering the demon-bound from captivity. He fed famished souls, undertook divine endorsed evangelistic crusades, writing of books, bringing healing to wounded souls, societies, nations and kingdoms in the world arena. He served about seven presidents of the United States of America as God's **emissary to the white house and to presidents.** His life was and is still a pinnacle of **righteous deeds. Righteousness Intelligence** will make you a Billy Graham. You will have access to presidents, secretary of states, federal secretaries, prime ministers, governors, mayors, bishops and world leaders.

In consonance with righteousness and flourishing, psalm 72: 7 asserts, "In *his days the righteous will flourish; prosperity will abound till the moon is no more.*" This important psalm was written by King Solomon exhorting kingdom citizens to beware of

---

[58] TBN, Santa Anna, California on November 8, 2012.

the reward of **righteousness.** Those who practiced righteousness during his reign were to flourish. The psalm also extends beyond the reign of King Solomon to embrace the Messianic Kingdom. Before the Parousia, those of us who are Christians are anointed and destined to prosper. If you are righteous, beware that you have the divine qualification to flourish. You are destined to flourish in your business, your family, in church, in whatever you do. Do you have **righteousness intelligence? Do you employ righteousness intelligence to prosper?** Then beware that the next few months prosperity and wealth will be your portion. Solomon believed in flourishing of the **righteous,** because he was wealthy himself. He wrote what he experienced as the most prosperous and wealthiest king ever to govern the United Kingdom of Israel. I exhort you to desire to have **righteous intelligence.** Over the years, I have grown to fathom that imbibing the word of God, engaging in fasting and prayer, fellowshipping with other believers, high-level educational pursuit, theological research, preaching and teaching the word of God, and **promptings of the Holy Spirit** have imbued me with **righteousness intelligence.**

Furthermore, proverbs 12: 12 categorically states, "The wicked desire the plunder of evil men, but the root of the righteous flourishes." Likewise proverbs 14: 11 asserts, "The house of the wicked will be destroyed, but the tent of the righteous will flourish." Similarly, proverbs 28:25 declares, "A greedy man stirs up dissensions, but he who trusts in the Lord will prosper. You have to comprehend that it is only the righteous person who trusts the Lord. He believes his Lord will step into that dicey situation and deliver him or her. The person believes strongly in the Lord's prosperity.

Most importantly, the person who wields *Righteousness intelligence* understands the significance of the *first fruit.* "Honor **the Lord with your wealth, with the first fruits of your crops; then your barns will be filled to overflowing, and your vats will brim over with new wine" (Pr. 3:9-10).** The first fruits were so significant for the community of Yahweh's people. It identified the people with their God. It determined the giving and benevolent attitude of the ordinary Israelite towards God. The person with **righteousness intelligence** will give his or her first fruits to God. What is the first fruit? **The first fruits were the best portions of their harvest. It was designated to God, for blessing them with a bumper harvest. It was in total gratitude of his manifold blessing throughout the faming season.** Deuteronomy 26:9-10 states, " He brought us to this place and gave us this land, a land flowing with milk and honey; and now I bring the **first fruits** of the soil that you, O Lord, have given me. Place the basket before the Lord your God and bow down before him."

Prosperity emanates from giving God your first fruits and worshipping him in the house of the Lord. Barns are reservoirs for storing farm produce. By offering the first fruits to God, the Israelites were assured of God's abundant blessings in the area of harvest, security, good health, honor and love. If you give him the best portion of your harvest, you will definitely prosper. The choicest wheat, corn, and grain was given to God. Likewise, the best and fattened animals such as lambs, cows, and fowls were offered to God in worship. In contextualization, it is appropriate for us to give the best part of our income to God. Give him one tenth of your weekly, biweekly or monthly income. Trust him and you will be rewarded. Giving to God first in our lives helps us to conquer greed, selfishness, egocentrism, or individualism. By placing God first in your giving, it helps you manage your resources. You definitely become a budgeter, budgeting for your family and for other expenditures.

I would want to exhort you not to give God your leftovers. God is not interested in your leftovers. He is interested in the first fruits. Do not offer anything that is worthless to God. Set aside the good portion of your harvest for the creator of heaven and earth.

## THE INTELLIGENCE OF COURAGE AND STRENGTH.

A courageous person is a leader. A courageous person possesses the Land. A courageous person has a heart of a lion and for that; matter has the heart of a champion. The courageous are the ones that succeed. A courageous personality is invincible. It takes the word of God coupled with the anointing of God to possess invincibility **intelligence of courage and strength.** Courage of heart **intelligence** is not associated with the stature of person; it is the substance and connectivity of the person to God. It is the synthesis of the whole personality; his or her mental impetus, academic training, spiritual formation, the call of God, Christocentric behavior as well as maturity of the person. A courageous person is imbued with social and ethical issues that constitute the life-wire of social and religious freedom, progress and acceptability. A courageous person speaks like a champion, and hence has words of victory. The wisdom of a courageous person cannot be challenged. Terror, calamities, setbacks, upheavals, turmoil, and danger are a watershed of fear, and doubt. Nevertheless, a courageous person overcomes them with the **command** of the Lord. Hence, scriptures asserts, "Have I not **commanded** you? Be strong and courageous. Do not be terrified; do not be discouraged, for the Lord your God will be with you wherever you go" (Joshua 1:9). Negativity engenders discouragement, discouragement generates doubt, doubt begets human strength, and human strength is always devoid of God and divine wisdom, and is bound to fail. There were several reasons why God **commanded** Joshua to be strong and courageous. In the first place, he was leading a stiff-necked people. They had a rebellious heart and were capable of rebelling against God and against his leadership. Earlier on, they rebelled against God and Moses in diverse ways and at several transitional places as they sojourned to the Promised Land. A leader without courage will melt in the face of opposition. Leadership without courage and strength is like building a skyscraper without a foundation. It takes the **courage and strength intelligence** to understand that to succeed in this perilous world, you must embrace **divine command** to be strong and courageous.

He needed the strength and courage **intelligence** in order to lead the recalcitrant people of Yahweh to the Promised Land. In Numbers 21:4-6 scripture states categorically, " **They traveled from Mount Hor along the route to the Red Sea, to go around Edom. But the people** grew impatient on the way; they spoke against God and against Moses, and said, why have you brought us up out of Egypt to die in the desert?. There is no bread! There is no water! And we detest this miserable food." Thus, Joshua needed a huge spiritual energy to lead the stiff-necked people of Yahweh to inherit the promised Land. An aspect of spiritual glucose that he really desired in order to lead the community of Yahweh people was **courage and Boldness.** Earlier on in Numbers 16:1-50, Korah, Dathan, and Abiram rose up against Moses and Aaron, when their oracular pronouncement belittled the leadership of Moses and Aaron. God poured out his wrath on them. The earth was split open and swallowed up **Korah, Dathan, and Abiram.** Next the 250 people who rebelled against God, Moses and Aaron and offered sacrifices were consumed by fire (verse 35). From verse 41 to 50, the congregation complained against Moses and Aaron again. God was so annoyed that he visited his judgement on the people. A plague consumed fourteen thousand, and seven hundred of them.

Furthermore, "The whole Israelite community set out from Elim and came to the Desert of Sin, which is between Elim and Sinai, on the fifteenth day of the second month after they had come out of Egypt.[2] In the desert the whole community grumbled against Moses and Aaron. [3] The Israelites said to them, "If only we had died by the LORD's hand in Egypt! There we sat around pots of meat and ate all the food we wanted, but you have brought us out into this desert to starve this entire assembly to death." Then the LORD said to Moses, "I will rain down bread from heaven for you. The people are to go out each day and gather enough for that day. In this way I will test them and see whether they will follow my instructions. [5] On the sixth day they are to prepare what they bring in, and that is to be twice as much as they gather on the other days" (Exodus 16:1-4). Having witnessed his predecessors Moses and Aaron in leadership battle with the people, God wanted him to master courage in order to lead his chosen people to inherit the promised Land that he had sworn to their forefathers.

Another reason why he desired this anointing and leadership

pep talk was to overcome archenemies, natural barriers, and fortified and versatile armies of neighboring tribes. With the command of God and with special leadership adroitness, he led the people to cross the Jordan River on a dry land (Joshua 3:1-17). An anointed leader is courageous, and audacious leaders perform miracles. Whatever is impossible for people, when you receive a command of leadership and victorious words from the Lord, you manifest undeniable miracles of God. While the Egyptians perished in the Red Sea, Moses and his people traversed over to the other side. While in the watching eyes of the world, it appeared impossible to cross the Jordan without sophisticated nautical dexterity, and sailing skills, Joshua performed a miracle; the waters stopped flowing and the Ark of the Covenant of the Lord, the priests, the elders and the whole congregation crossed on a dry land to the opposite side of the Jordan River.

Having received **leadership, courage and strength intelligence,** he and the congregation marshaled up military, and theocratic prayer momentum to bring down the Jericho wall. Jericho that posed as a threat and obstacle to their journey and prosperity was overcome (Joshua 5:13-15; 6:1-27). Courage and strength **intelligence,** which emanates from the Lord wields you the military power to engage in the impossibility. The Jericho wall was a fortified military barrack. It was a rampart of all ancient times, an impregnable edifice that could not be brought down by any technological research of their time. The flaming arrow, the fiercest military weapon had little or no effect on the might of the wall, even if it was thrown against it. Nevertheless, courage and strength coupled with leadership anointing quaked the foundation of the fortified wall making it tumbled in the face of Yahweh people.

Notwithstanding crossing the Jordan River, and hauling down the Jericho wall, Joshua and the congregation had a daunting mission of vanquishing versatile and famous kings. Hence, he had to be strong and courageous in order to annihilate the territory of Og, king of Bashan. He reigned in mount Hebron, taking control of the Western Corridor of the River Jordan. He was defeated with the leadership skills of Joshua. Sihon, king of the Amorites was also defeated with the **intelligence of courage.** Thus, Joshua and the Israelites conquered the following kings: **The king of Jericho, the king of Ai (near Bethel), the king of Jerusalem, the king of Hebron, the King of Jarmuth, the king of Lachish, the king of Eglon, the king of Gezer (Joshua 12:1-12).** He conquered the western foothill, the Hittities, the Amorites, Canaanites, Perizzites, Hivites, and Jebusites. He also conquered important cities in the north such as Hazor. In total, Joshua and the people of Yahweh overpowered the land both East (Joshua 12:1-6) and the west (Joshua 12: 7- 27) of the Jordan River. They defeated 31 kings and their cities. With military dexterity coupled with courage and strength **intelligence,** the Israelites vanquished the Hittites, the Amorites, the Canaanites, the Prizzites, the Hivites, and the Jebusites. A person permeated with **courage and strength intelligence** overpowers the financial barriers, work related barriers, political, social, and marital hurdles. With economic meltdown and governments struggling with the **fiscal cliff,** Christians desire the invincibility of the Lord to survive the turbulent times. They need the command of **courage and strength intelligence to eschew mortgage crises, to stem out the venom of unemployment,** to revamp their businesses and to be extricated form poverty, enslavement and contempt. You cannot really possess your **"promised Land"** if you woefully lack **courage and strength intelligence.** Those kings and their people were versatile warriors who knew the military terrain of all territories but with the Lord, the Israelites overcame them. You need the Lord to overpower undesirable kings, undesirable financial embarrassments, nauseating family woes, intellectual and religious belittlement.

In the final exhortation of King David to the heir and prince to the throne of Israel as a theocratic State, he explicates to Solomon, **"Then you will have success if you are careful to observe the decrees and laws that the lord gave Moses for Israel. <u>Be strong and courageous. Do not be afraid or discouraged"</u> (1 chronicles 22:13).** Apart from observing the Mosaic Law and decrees, which constituted national blue print for success, David also exhorted Solomon to be **strong and courageous.** It takes a courageous person to lead people of diverse emotional stamina, tribal, and national affiliation, and psychological position with the Lord. The twenty-first century is a cosmos of cosmopolitan religious entity, consisting of people of divergent cultures, financial classes, racial affiliations, and ethnic relations. The people of Israel were divided into twelve tribes with tribal problems. Moreover, since Solomon was to lead and administer justice (mishpat) to everyone without favor, he needed the **intelligence of courage and strength.** David knowing the **significance** of **courage and strength** instructed his beloved son to be courageous, and to avoid fear. It takes an anointed king to pass onto the next generation the invincibility of God's word and command. The successes of the next generations of the twenty-first century depend solely on the current leadership and those passing the leadership baton to the next generations. Virtue, intelligence, leadership dexterity, technological inventions, pastoral training, academic zenith of all times, business acumen, social reconstruction in the dimension of socio-economic landscape are needed to reshape the future of world societies.

In addition, *"David also said to Solomon his son, be strong and courageous, and do the work. Do not be afraid, or discouraged, for the Lord God, my God, is with you. He will not fail you or forsake you until all the work for the service of the Temple of the Lord is finished" (1Chrinicles 28: 20).* Fear destroys visions and dreams, but courage and strength fulfills visions and dreams. Fear generates doubt, which leads to defeat, but courage and strength are a foundation stone for success. In building the magnificent Temple, Solomon needed to be strong and courageous. Courage and strength were intertwined in the anointing of royalty. You cannot succeed in accomplishing your dreams and visions if you woefully lack strength and courage. It takes courage and strength to construct a magnificent edifice that towers above every building in the kingdom. It takes courage to carve out an image of glory for oneself and for the kingdom of God. It takes courage to dare the impossible. Even David as a little boy imbued with the spirit of courage slew the seemingly impossible philistine warrior, Goliath. With courage, you destroy the intellectual, as well as the military power of your adversaries. It takes divine courage to possess what is due you. You cannot build your personal reputation, your family, church, and community without courage. Courage and strength are virtues that emanate from the spirit and heart of the individual. It is not drug overdosed foolish strength. Carnality and human strength is the root cause of decimation and unfathomable calamities. Your dreams and visions must be orchestrated using the word and the anointing of God. It suffices to say that strength and courage are a watershed of victory. Actually, the two are the epicenter of victory. They are the wellspring of joy, happiness, and immeasurable breakthroughs. With courage and strength, you will not fail. With courage, you know that God will not forsake you.

In the New Testament, Paul entreats his audience to be strong in the Lord and in the power of his might. Paul is exhorting them to find their strength in the Lord. They need to draw constantly upon the power they already possess through their union with Christ. To be strong in the Lord is further explained by the phrase, "and in the power of his might." Power denotes an active force, whereas might denotes a passive force, inherently possessed whether exercised or not. To be strong in the Lord denotes that the believer needs to be made aware that the battle is for the Lord himself who has already dealt a deadly blow to the forces of evil.[59]. The things that are commanded are impossible to perform without God's strength and grace. We need his strength and power to overcome our enemies, our flesh, and Satan. We need his strength to adorn the doctrine of Christ with holiness and integrity. Even though we are weak and can do nothing by ourselves, his grace is sufficient for all things.[60]The call "to be strong" in the face of a severe battle is prototype of Old Testament scriptures, the most obvious refers to Joshua, who was commanded "to be strong and of good courage" (Joshua 1: 6-7,

---

[59] Willard .H Taylor. *Beacon Bible expositions: Galatians and Ephesians* (Kansas City: Beacon Hill Press, 1982), 209.

[60] Henry T. Maham. *Bible class Commentary* (England: Evangelical Press, 1991), 68.

9). Correspondingly, David also found strength in the Lord when the Amalekites invaded Ziklag (1 Sam 30:6). When the remnants returned from the Babylonian captivity, God declared, "I will make them strong in the Lord (Zech. 10:12).[61]

## Prayer involves Forgiveness

One of the most terrible diseases that everybody grapples with in life is the inability to forgive. It is a known fact that where forgiveness is lacking the spiritual as well as the physical atmosphere becomes chaotic. Since the time of creation the inability of nations, individuals, groups of people as well as various religious faiths to forgive one another has caused humanity a great deal of harm than good. Inability to forgive has engendered wars among nations. It has also succeeded in causing a wanton decimation of communities, friends, ethnic groups, and families. Nations rise against nations, family members turn against each other, and blood is shed in every passing minute because someone has blatantly refused to forgive and has taken the law into their own hands.

Un-forgiveness is as poisonous as the viper's udder. It paralyzes the nervous system and kills its victim either spiritually or physically. Satan knowing its potency uses it to cause havoc in marriages and in the society. What then is forgiveness? Forgiveness is described as the "act of setting someone free from an obligation to you that is as a result of wrong done to you." For example, a debt is forgiven when you free your debtor of his obligation to pay back what he owes you. Forgiveness therefore consists of three important words. Someone or both are *injured,* then a *debt* resulting from the injury, and *cancellation* of the debt. For forgiveness to take place, the injured

[61] Peter T. Obrian, *The Letter to the Ephesians* (Grand Rapids, Michigan: William B. Eerdmans, 1999), 461. Peter T. obrian further elucidates that the apostle might have been thinking of Is. 40:26 as he wrote Eph. 6:10 since the terms *kratos and lochuos* are related to this Old Testament passage, and hence the author is indebted to Isaiah for his terms and metaphors.

must make a conscious effort to release the offender of his debt by canceling all the hurts she or he has meted out to the injured. It deals with the turbulent internal reaction. It is a deliberate decision enabled by the spirit of God not to harbor anger and resentment against the offender. It is a deliberate decision to forget it, erase it off your heart, and Let it go. Forgiveness will benefit us for a number of reasons. It will prevent anger, resentment, and rancor from taking root in our hearts. It prevents retaliations such as denial of certain individual rights, abduction, homicide, and murder, which are characteristics of un-forgiveness. It also gives us the peace and tranquility that we need to serve our God. It even paves way for our prayers to be answered by God.

Everyone is encouraged to eschew this terminal disease called "un-forgiveness" by mapping out spiritual strategies that will eventually pave way for them to forgive whatever offences committed against them. One of the cardinal reasons for the incarnation of Jesus is to make every believer enjoy LIFE and have it ABUNDANTLY and not to enjoy life in pieces. *The thief cometh not, but for to steal, and to kill, and to destroy: I am come that they might have life, and that they might have it more abundantly (John 10:10).* Are you ready to enjoy life fully as Jesus has promised all believers? Then you must make a concerted effort by being rooted in the word of God. You need to work assiduously to fill every valley, clear every mountain, and dislodge every impediment on your way in order to enjoy this LIFE to the full. One single important way of achieving this is to forgive and forget.

Paul says, *Brothers, I do not consider myself yet to have taken hold of it. However, one thing I do: Forgetting what is behind and straining toward what is ahead. I press on toward the goal to win the prize for which God has called me heaven ward in Christ Jesus" (Ph3: 13-14).*Paul sees himself as a runner in a race exerting all his energy and pressing on with intense concentration in order not to fall short of the goal that Christ has set for his life. A determination of this caliber is necessary for all of us. In our Christian journey, there is no doubt that all kinds of distractions and temptations, such as worries about life, materialism and evil desires threaten to choke our commitment to the Lord. This verse also educates that what is needed is to forget behind the corrupt world and our old life of sin. Paul was an archenemy of the Christian faith. He fiercely persecuted the Church and endorsed the assassination of Stephen. However, he realized that thinking about those negative achievements was not going to yield any dividend for him. Have you faulted in one way other? Forget about it and look ahead. Have you ever failed in business or due to an infantile behavior landed your relationship or marriages on rocks? Forget about the past, and concentrate on the future. You can make your home a paradise again if you desire to change things around. Forget about what is behind and make an effort to reach out for what is ahead.

Many people wrestle with the idea of maintaining a good relationship or restoring a relationship that has fallen apart because of failure to release the past. The past is a killer of joy, an enemy of progress and destroyer of purposes and visions. You cannot live in the past mistakes and expect to achieve anything meaningful in the future. You should understand that the past blunders, and offenses exist only in memory. They only have power over you if you continue to give immaturity the power to operate. Do not brood over the past. Let it go. Release it, move freely, and declare that you are not your past. If you do not release the past, it will pounce on you as a venomous python overpowers its prey. The enemy of the new is the old. No matter how bad your past was, it could not be compared with the glory of your present and future. You have to fight against the past mistakes, disappointment, and betrayals. In athletics, a competitor who is fond of looking back is most likely to be overtaken by his opponents. Turning to look back pulls, you back; it does not push you forward. Never break down with your failures, and mistakes. Until you make a conscious effort to forgive, your future will not resurrect. ***Resentment is a bulldog bite that clenches the teeth of memory into the dead past and refuses to let go.*** Nevertheless, painful experiences must be accepted emotionally as well as rationally so that there can be restoration in relationships. For instance, in marriage, each spouse should be ready to say, *"I finish my demands on your past acts and words, now let us live together in peace and not in pieces."*

## FORGIVENESS MAKES PRAYERS EFFECTIVE

Prayer and forgiveness are intertwined in the New Testament. In Matthew 6: 14-15, Jesus taught His disciples how to pray. Then in Mark 11:22-24, he educated His disciples the command of Faith and the prayer of faith. The next two verses are expository note on forgiveness giving a prominence to His previous statement on prayer by declaring, *"And when you stand praying, if you hold anything against anyone, forgive him, so that your father in heaven may forgive you your sins. (Mark 11:25-26).* Likewise, He educated His disciples by both instruction and parable in Matthew 18: 21-35). In this context his expository teaching on forgiveness is directly linked to his afore instruction on prayer. The Bible is the inspired word of God, and none of these textual linkups are by no means accidental but divinely planned to help Christians overcome some obstacles in their lives and to help others overcome similar hurdles.

The theme of prayer and forgiveness in these passages are not autonomous but inseparably associated. If you want your prayer to be answered, you must forgive. You adamantly refuse to let go the offences meted out to you by someone; your cry for help will not be attended to. We will receive nothing if we harbor resentment, rancor, and acrimony towards any soul. Forgiving your neighbor of their sins will propel the hand of God to forgive you in all your endeavors.

Furthermore, **Forgiveness gives you advantage over Satan.** In his epistle to the Corinthian Church, Paul exhorts His addressees to be wary of the dangers of failing to forgive. *"If you forgive anyone, I also forgive him. In addition, what I have forgiven- if there was anything to forgive- I have forgiven in the sight of Christ for your sake, in order that Satan might not outwit us. For we are not unaware of* *his schemes" (2 Corinthians 2: 10-11).* In this passage, Paul made it clear that Satan would gain an upper hand over them in their battle against him if they failed to forgive. He would manipulate power, and have the competence to seduce, influence, and exert control over their lives.

# CHAPTER 6

## HOW TO ARISE AND SHINE I CHRONICLES 4:9

The Bible is replete with men and women who took action to turn their seemingly impossible situations around. Anything that took place in somebody's life meant that they arose and did something positive about it. King Hezekiah prevailed in prayer to rescue his life from the jaws of death, King David prayed, sought counsel for his own life and the life of Israel when enemies came against him. Zacheous, the hated and infamous publican did something about his life to have his story and name recorded in the Bible. Bartimaus rose up and ran towards Jesus. That action delivered him from the shackles of social stigma and blindness. The two blind men cried out to Jesus saying, "Have mercy on us son of David" (Mt.9:27). Their cry brought them deliverance. Their physical blindness and myopia was restored . They spiritual position changed to embrace the glory of God. Their social stigmatization and rejection erased and paved way for them to be reintegrated into the society. Time **does not always** solve problems; rather it is the application of relevant truth that solves problems. "May God arise, may his enemies be scattered; may his foes flee before him" (Ps 68:1). This psalm celebrates God's rule over and care for the people of Israel and his victory over His enemies. It may also foreshadow Christ destruction of the evil one at the end of age, and the triumph of all believers in Christ, as we rejoice eternally in God's presence. Every advancement in life attracts storms or challenges. To make your goals, purposes and dreams be materialized, you need to stand firm in the Lord. No problem can solve itself until you arise to fight it.

JABEZ was born under unfavorable circumstances. The mother named him Jabez; she gave birth to him in **pain**. The synonyms for pain are **discomfort, agony, aching, hurt, ache, sting, soreness, throbbing, smarting, stinging, twinge and hurting.** The name meant that he was destined to live in agony or hurt for his entire life. The unfavorable situation in which he found himself was not his own making. He did not choose to be born into that family. He did not request his mother to say indecent words about him. Actually, he was born into sorrow and he grew up before he knew that his future was under severe threat. Strikingly, he refused to embrace the unfavorable circumstances confronting him at that moment rather; he did something spectacular about his life.

## He refused to live in Sorrow

He made a choice about his future. In Deuteronomy 30: 19 Moses exhorted the people of Israel to choose life and live. *"This day I call heaven and earth as witnesses against you that I have set before you life and death, blessing and curses. Now choose life, so that you and your children may live."* He took responsibility for his life. Excuse is a fertile ground for failures and setbacks. Responsibility is the rule of the game. He confronted his limitation. Nobody can make your life better than you can. Think your way through. He refused to blame his mother, nor his father, uncles, bothers, and sisters. Complaining spirit is a deadly spirit. It plants impediments in your way; it does not propel you into achieving your goals and dreams. It drags you into the quagmire of life, it does not uplift you. It grieves you; it does not give you joy. It curses you; it does not bless you. It demotes you; it does not promote you. This deadly spirit delayed and prolonged the Israelites' journey for forty years. This cancerous spirit keeps you busily talking about things not done and prevents you taking steps to address situations.

## HE WAS HONORABLE

He was honorable than his brothers, may be due to the nature of his prayers. He was being earnest, which means, intense, zealous, sincere, and determined. The Hebrew word is **kabed, or kabed** meaning *abounding, achieve honor, distinguished,* and *burdensome* depending on the context. It meant that Jabez was more **distinguished** than his brothers. He was more respected by God and people in his neighborhood than his brothers. The **Aramaic** lexical item for honorable is **yaqqir** whose connotation is the same as that of Hebrew, **honorable or difficult.** The fifth of the Ten Commandments: *"Honor your father and your mother so that your days be lengthened on the land that I give you (EX.20:12).* In other words, *"honor"* means treating one's parents with the gravity that their position demands. In one of many examples of the genius of Torah Hebrew, the opposite of "honor" is "kalel." The word is always translated as "to curse." The Bible clearly states in James 5: 16 that "the effective fervent prayer of a righteous man avails much." The second aspect that made him honorable was humility. Humility is a key to becoming honorable in every endeavor of life. "Humble yourself, therefore, under God's mighty hand, that he may lift you up in due time. Cast all your anxiety on him because he cares for you (1 Peter 5: 6-7). Paul declares, I served the Lord with great humility and with tears, although I was severely tested by the plots of the Jews." (Acts 20:19). Jesus the second person of the Trinity humbled himself. "And being found in appearance as a man, he humbled himself and became obedient to death- even death on the cross." (Phil 2:8). Humility was a virtue that made Jabez honorable. According to the author of **The Millionaire Mind,** Dr. Thomas J. Stanley, an important factor for high-level success in business and one's positive endeavors is **honesty.** He affirms in his masterpiece that not anyone, who lacks integrity or honesty, should ever graduate into economic success. People, who are honest wield high moral values, which are incorruptible. An honorable person is able to dichotomize between right and wrong, falsification of facts and veracity of facts. In summation, in business people with high-level moral integrity and honest succeed in becoming millionaires. Likewise, Jabez was a man of honor, a man of integrity. His lifestyle was tailored according to the moral standards of God. In fact, he was incorruptible.[62]

## HE WAS MONOTHEISTIC IN PRAYER

He directed his prayer to God alone. Jesus in Matt 6: 9 educates all Christians to direct their prayers to God only by declaring, *"Our father in heaven, hollowed be your name."* The word "Father" or "ancestor" is derived from the Hebrew expression *"ab."* It is used as the address of small and adult children to their fathers. It was a respectful and honorable address to even the matured.[63] In Jewish prayer, there are many derivatives of the address of God as Father, such as *abii* "my father", or *abiinu* "our Father". Therefore, *ab* in this context is characterized by the central idea of fervent relationship, a rapport of intimacy, and the loving kindness of God[64]. Jabez had a fervent relationship with his God, and so he called on him only. This intimate connection applies to every person especially "those who are born of the Spirit of God" (Gal 4:6; Mark 14:36). Scripture states, "For you did not receive a spirit that makes you a slave again to fear, but you receive the spirit of sonship, and by him we cry Abba Father" (Rom 8:15). Thus, the Lord's Prayer is a prayer of the children

---

[62] 54 Thomas J. Stanley, *The Millionaire Mind* (Kansas City: Andrews Mcmeel Publishing, 2000), 52.

[63] Robert H. Gundry, Matthew: *A Commentary on His Literary and Theological Art* (Grand Rapids, Michigan: William B. Eerdmans, 1982), 105.

[64] Page H. Kelley, *Biblical Hebrew: An Introductory Grammar* (Grand Rapids, Michigan, William B. Eerdmans, 1992), 6.

of God that is the citizens of the New Israel. It absolutely confirms the covenantal relationship between God the Father and us, his children.

Even the psalmist declares, *"I lift up my eyes to the hills- where does my help come from? My help comes from the Lord, the maker of heaven and earth."* (Psalm 121:1). Another psalmist declares in Psalm 91: 2 *"I will say of the Lord, He is my refuge and my fortress, my God in whom I trust."* To direct your prayers to God alone means to depend on him alone for all your needs. "Do not be anxious about anything, but in everything by prayer and petition, with thanksgiving, present your requests to God. And the peace of God, which transcends all understanding, will guard your hearts and your minds in Christ Jesus" (Phil 4:6-7). Jabez did not consult the Baal or any of the gods of the surrounding nations. He could have traveled to those lands for divinations and consultations of mediums, but he chose to direct his prayer to the monotheistic God. He refused to be polytheistic in his attitude towards God. Refuse to consult a psyche or any idol but enthusiastically anchor your faith in God and the results of your faithfulness will be marvelous.

The First commandment clearly states, "You shall have no other gods" (Ex.20:3-6). Other gods depict fabricated gods usually carved out of stones and wood and worshipped by other nations that encompassed Israel. The command educates that God is a jealous God who does not tolerate spiritual apostasy. He is a personal God who requires genuine believers to develop a high-level personal relationship with him. Therefore, to venerate an image of God instead of God himself who created *(bara)* man and woman in his own image is sacrilegious. In Judges 2:10, we are well-informed that an entire generation was thrown into oblivion because of gross neglect of their parents. "Another generation grew up which knew neither the Lord nor what the Lord had done for Israel...then the Israelites followed and worshipped other gods." As a result, the children were severely punished until they were sent to exile in (2 Kgs 25). Moreover, because they worshipped other gods and were stiff-necked as their parents, the Lord was very angry with Israel and removed them from his presence (2 Kgs 17:7-18). Jabed knew the consequence of apostasy, hence he refused to worship other gods or direct his prayer to them. He fastened his faith in God alone, the creator of heaven and the earth. Do not be tempted to consult a psyche or be involved in divinations and witchcraft manipulations in the name of postmodern culture. It is abhorrence to God. To shine and overcome all manners of debilitation issues confronting you, you must direct your prayer to the supreme commander of the universe only. Jabez did so and the results were marvelous. We shall not flag or fail. We shall go on to the end. - Winston Churchill

## HE CRIED TO THE LORD FOR HELP

In addition, he cried to God for help. He turned to God in prayer and in supplication for deliverance. He cried out to the God of Israel, "Oh that you would bless me and enlarge my territory." Turn to God for help and stop complaining and grumbling. Do not shift blames but rather do something to salvage your situation. Prov 18:20-21 *"A man's belly shall be satisfied with the fruit of his mouth; and with the increase of his lips shall he be filled. Death and life are in the power of the tongue: and they that love it shall eat the fruit thereof."* The tongue is one of the channels through which we receive our blessings. A proper use of the tongue will yield blessings for us while a wrong use of the tongue will bring us curses. Before you cry to man, cry to God first. Before you take the matter to man, take it to God first. Before you make somebody to dine with you with your challenges, dine with God first. Jabez in the wisdom of God requested for a personal blessing and favor from God. Psalm 28: 9 declares, "Save your people and bless your inheritance, be their shepherd and carry them forever." Enlarging his territory denotes material blessing. After seeking the kingdom of God, the next step is to request God for material blessing. He implored that God's hand would be upon him. He cried for the protection, guidance of God upon his life. "Guide me in your truth and teach me, for you are God my savior, and my hope is in you all day long." (Psalm 25:5). Why did he pray such a prayer? That he might not cause pain. A commentator states, "Let me not experience the grief which my name implies and which my sins would well produce." Another commentator idealized it, "grant that the grief implied in my name may not come upon me." Psalm 119:31 states, "I hold fast to your status, O Lord; do not let me be put to shame." Jabez prayed that the magnitude of negativity associated with his name would not befall him. Prayer has the potency to extricate you from ancestral curses as well as the curse of the tongue. He cried to his God to receive deliverance and unfathomable blessings. You can also cry to your God for manifold blessings of the Lord. You can overcome **21st Century** problems by calling on God to enlarge your territory.

## PRAYER WILL FORTIFY YOU IN TIMES OF TRIALS AND TEMPTATION

Prayer strengthens you in times of trials and Temptations. Trials actually involve philosophical analyses in the sense that their main objective is to bring out what is actually embedded in the individual. Trials in themselves are not bad per se but are to unravel the good in us. Trials test us so that what we are composed of is made evident to all, as to whether we consist of gold or straw. Trials in our lives will determine the kind of substance we are made up of. In James 1:2-4, the author, outlines the importance of trials. Trials lead to the development of perseverance and wisdom. *"My brothers, count it joy when you fall in diverse temptations; knowing this that the trying of your faith worketh patience.*

While the humble will overcome trials and prove that they are made of valuable substance, the rich will always find it extremely difficult to survive the trials that come their way. Chapter one verses 9-11 and 5: 1-6 illustrate this kind of judgment coming upon the rich. As the sun withers the grass and the flowers falls of, so shall the rich fall away in his ways. This means that we have to eschew every form of pride and adopt a humble attitude towards God and humanity.

There are also rewards for being resolute under the trial. This is because it brings so much joy, peace, and tranquility when we fall into diverse temptations and are able to endure them. Actually, the same word is used for trial and temptation in verse 2 of chapter one. peirasmoz, *peirasmos*, is used to refer to both *trials, and temptations.* The word **peirasmos** in James 1:2, and James 1:12-13 is worthy of explanation. The word is extremely difficult to define since it is only meaning potential. The word is a symbol waiting for a context to be defined or interpreted. The meaning of **peirasmos** can only be ascertained by relating it to other words in the context. In three consecutive contexts, the word portrays different connotations. In James 1:2 **peirasmos** means a "trial", which is defined further as *"a testing of your faith"* in verse 3. In verse 13, however, the meaning of **peirasmos** evolves into another semantic range, which is *"**temptation.**"* The statement, "God is tempting me" which engenders the discussion on the source of temptation and its consequences, engineers the shift in semantic domain. Hence, the meaning was not an embodiment of **peirasmos** but was defined in context. In Linguistics, the term **peirasmos** may be defined as a grammatical word since its connotation in the last explanation is anchored in context and not in the word form itself. Usually, a preposition, a conjunction, or an article functions as a grammatical word in Linguistics theory. Therefore, whosoever overcomes, will receive the crown of life at the end of the age. Temptation has the tendency of making the victim to fall and deviate from the righteousness of God. Like trials, temptations have their sources. According to James, 1: 13-18, the tempter is not God. God does not tempt people, because he is not evil to orchestrate such a diabolical act against his chosen ones. Nevertheless, every man is tempted when he allows his own lust to tempt and entice him. Lust thus, when fully conceived, engenders sin and when sin is fully-grown gives birth to death. The **key** to overcome trials and Temptation is **fasting and prayer, self-controlled, the word of God and maturity.**

## PRAYER WILL HELP YOU SUBDUE
## MORAL CONFLICT

The moral conflict approach postulates that within every individual there is a struggle between the *id* and the *super ego*. The *id* mostly is found in children who are instinct driven. It is an individualistic instinct that drives the person into self-pleasing behavior. The superego on the other hand is the voice of the authority figure in the adult's life. It is the internalization of rewards and punishment. Thus, in adult life, the adult reason tries to deal with the conflict between the *id* and the super ego. If an adult fails to solve problems using the super ego he will resort to defensive mechanism, repression, ascetism, isolation, displacemt, turning against the self, projection and interjection.

It is obvious that from Genesis to Revelation, individuals and group of people have often grappled with moral choices. They are caught up in the cross roads of either to please God or to please their individualistic desires. For example, Adam and Eve were faced with the Moral choice of either eating the fruit or obeying God. In Gerer, Abraham, faced the moral decision as to speak the truth or tell a lie about his wife. King David was confronted with the moral choice between committing adultery with Beersheba and killing Uriah or avoiding murder and sacrilegious sexual relationship with her in order to have an invincible kingdom. To mention but a few, Ananias and Saphira faced with the moral decision as to please their self-centered instincts or to obey the Holy Spirit. Peter was confronted with the moral choice whether to deny Jesus three times and be made a worthless leader to to acknowledge Jesus as his savior and be made invincible. Judas Iscariot was confronted with the moral choice of selling Jesus for 30 silver coins for evanescent goods, and losing his life or remain faithful to him and obtain eternal life. Those who are still children in their Christian walk must be taught to grow up in their faith with God. Prayer is a foundation stone to overcoming a myriad of problems. Jesus teaches us to pray that we may be spared failures, difficulties and even overcome them. To overcome self-centered actions, which we do not want God to interfere, the presence of the spirit may be restored when we repent and ask God for restoration. *"If you return to the Lord with all your heart, remove your foreign gods. From among you and direct your hearts to the Lord. He will deliver you"* (1 Sam 7:3). Directing our hearts towards God is repentance that we change our mind and heart about sin and about God. When people repent and do away with earthly dependencies and allow God's presence to abide in their lives they can change. This is because God's abundance grace draws near to them. Repentance will change behavior because it changes the heart. Prayer fortifies the believer against perilous issues confronting him or her in the 21st Century. prayer must be embraced as a cornerstone for success and deliverance. Prayer coupled with sound biblical counseling and teaching will illuminate your mind and heart so that you will make divine directed choices. Our choices determine our success level. If we make choices based on the *id*, we may suffer failures but if our choices are anchored in the *superego*, we are mostly like to be placed on the pedestal of success. Prayer is the **key** to success.

# CHAPTER 7

## TAMING THE TONGUE (JAMES 3: 1-12)

James in this awesome chapter warns us of the potentially and destructive power of human speech. Our words have enormous spiritual impact on our life. The tongue even though small has influence out of proportion t to its diminutive size. The new man in Christ has a new mouth, a new tongue, and a new speech. In view of this, the tongue becomes the litmus test for the heart. In chapter 1: 26, James says, "If any man among you seems to be religious, or thinks himself to be religious, or presents himself as being religious, but does not bridle heart, he is deceiving his own heart and his religion is useless. Therefore, when James speaks of the tongue, he speaks of the truth that the tongue will reveal the heart condition and at the same time calls us to do everything in our capacity to control it. A spiritually mature person will use the tongue with discretion, weighing what is being said. Ephesians 4: 29 states " Do not let any unwholesome talk come out of your mouths, but only what is helpful for building others up according to their needs, that it may benefit those who listen.

## THE TONGUE MUST BE CONTROLLED BECAUSE IT HAS THE POWER TO CONTROL (V. 2-5)

The tongue has the potency to control humanity. If the tongue were not controlled, it would control everything in the world. The **Metaphor of the bit is** used in this context to illustrate the might of the tongue. The bit that controls the horse in verse 3 illustrates that something small has the effectiveness to manipulate something gigantic. This was the order of the day in the olden times. When a bit is put in the mouth of horses, we can control them easily. We can persuade them for our benefit and as a result, we can turn the whole animal. Thus, the tongue has the ability to determine the destiny of the individual. Believers who are able to control the tongue have the aptitude to direct the course of the whole body or person thereby making it perfect in the end. However, when the tongue is not used with discretion, the rest of the body is likely to be unrestrained and disruptive leading to pandemonium lifestyle. Therefore, to profit from the smallest organ of the human body in terms of spiritual illustrations, the 21st century believer must use the tongue with decorum.

**Another metaphor used is the rudder** illustrated in verse.4; it is the rudder that steers the ship. The rudder even though small controls the large ship. It has the competence to control that large and bulky structure of a ship. It gearshifts the ship in the midst of strong, harsh, rough, cruel winds or storms. **Aristotle,** states, one man turns the small size of the ruder so that a huge mass of a ship is controlled. Thus, the tongue has tremendous power to control. Just as the bit controls the horse, the tongue also controls the body. It is like a rudder, even though very small control a huge ship. The tongue is a small member, it boasts about great things. Why must we control the tongue? Because it is the leader in sinning. We sin with it more frequently than any part of our body. We must control the tongue because it has potential to condemn and its power to control. It dominates a person and is a key to their behavior.

Furthermore, **the tongue has the power to corrupt (V.5&6).**

Even though it is very small, it boats about great things. It has a fearful influence of annihilation. A forest is set ablaze by such a small fire. You can use one little tiny butt of cigarette and set thousands and tens of thousands of acres on fire. A spark of fire can raise a city down. If you have a cup of water and you pour it down, it will not become a river, spring, dam, sea or ocean but if you have a match or a coal of fire, a single spark can bring down a city. The tongue is like fire, what it says has an enormous effect. Verse 6 says the tongue is a fire; it is a WORLD OR SYSTEM, A COSMOS OF INIQUITY.

It is the system of iniquity. The tongue is an iniquitous system. A potential evil falls short of the glory of God. Its behavioral unrighteousness is within man. It inflames all the capacities of the person to bring the person into wicked system. No bodily organ has such an enormous potential for calamities as the tongue. The tongue defiles the entire body. It is like smoke from fire staining everything. Proverbs 15: 28 asserts, "The mouth of the wicked pours out wicked evil things." Proverbs 16:27 "An ungodly man digs up evil and in his lips there is a burning fire". Everything his fiery mouth touches is set on fire and the fire spreads. Proverbs 26: 20 "where no wood is, there the fire goes out. Where there is no talebearer, the strife ceases. The person who passes wicked reports, gossip or slander or a lie is like the wood that fuels the fire. Proverbs 26: 21 " But as coals to burning coals and wood to fire, so is a contentious man to **KINDLE** strife." The picture is that gossip, slander, and contention are all fire that has the potential to cause havoc. Psalm 52: 2 "The tongue devises mischief like a razor. Yes, the tongue is like a razor, it cuts. PSALM 64:1-2"Hear me, O God, as I voice my complaint; protect my life from the threat of the enemy. Hide me from the conspiracy of the wicked, from that noisy and crowd of evildoers. They sharpen their tongues like swords and aim their words like deadly arrows.

Homogeneously, your tongue holds the key to your life. Your mouth determines the result of every battle. You can be extricated from the shackles of poverty and sicknesses through the power of the spoken word. *"A man's belly shall be satisfied with the fruit of his mouth; and with the increase of his lips shall he be filled"*

*(Prv.18:22).* There is no doubt that positive confessions pave way for fruitful and optimistic lifestyle. For instance, your marriage can resurrect to the amazement of everyone through the words you speak into it. If you desire to win back what you incurred in your life, speak the word of God into the situation. If you consciously and faithfully apply this method to your daily life, you will marvel at the results. The way you speak to your spouse will determine the behavior he or she will put up. The way you describe your spouse is what you will receive. Scriptures cannot be broken; God performs miracles through the spoken word. Actually, no foul language should be ascribed to one's spouse. Progress in every endeavor is achieved via the positive use of the tongue. Do you want your spouse to embrace you, kiss you, and say honey; I love you, then imbibe the word of God and apply it to your marriage. The Bible says, a soft tongue breaks the bone. It means that you can overcome many difficulties by appropriately using the tongue. If there has ever been a verbal assault on your spouse, apologize to him or her and reverse all those utterances in the name of Jesus. If you confess poverty, you will have it as your bedmate, if you confess brightness and intelligence, wisdom and the favor of God; you will have them as your allies. *"A man's belly shall be satisfied with the fruit of his mouth; and with the increase of his lips shall he be filled."*(Proverbs 18: 20 says).

Unvaryingly, your words have creative abilities. In Genesis 1 and 2, God created the Universe through a spoken world. When God started the creation process, the earth was void and formless. God created the heavens and the earth from nothing (***creatio ex nihilo***) and he succeeded in doing so without placing numerous or severe demands on his very omnipotence or energy. He did not require preexistence substance in the creation process. He spoke and the universe was created. The Bible states, "By *the word of the LORD were the heavens made, their starry host by the breath of his mouth. For he spoke, and it came to be; he commanded, and it stood firm"* (Psalm 33: 6, 9). From the first day to the fifth day, God created the universe, while God created man in his own image (***imago Dei)*** on the sixth day. Because of carrying his divine image, Adam and Eve were commanded to have dominion over creation. They were perceptible depiction of God in his entire creation. Words used wisely in prayer have the ability to create your business, and your personal image. The words you speak possess the dynamites to create a new dimension of your family as well as your endeavors. God created the universe via the spoken word. You can create a new business by using the tongue wisely.

## PRAYER INVOLVES REBUKING THE ENEMY

Jesus was a healer, and had incomparable authoritative qualities. Moreover, as healer, he carried the landmarks of an exorcist as illustrated in the Gospel of Mark 1:21-27. Jesus cast out unclean Spirit by sternly rebuking the spirit to leave the victim's system. He also taught the people in the synagogue as one who had an incredible authority and not like scribes. Jesus used two most important words in this incident. First, *epitiman,* "rebuke". This word corresponds to the Hebrew or Aramaic word *"gaar"* or *gaw-ar* in its phonetic transcription. In Malachi 3:11, the word is used in the context of God restraining swarm of locusts. This word occurs 28 times in the Bible, 21 of them referring to the annihilation of the enemies of God. The word rebuke means *reprimand, strongly warn, restrain, reprove, chide.*The second word *epitimesen* "be silent", "to muzzle" occurs once in the Septuagint (LXX) as a translation of the Hebrew in Deut 25:4, where it refers to the muzzling of an ox. This expression is also used by Paul in 1 Tim 5:18. The Bible categorically states that Jesus "rebuked the wind and said to the waves, Quite! Be still. Then the wind died down and it was completely calm" (Mark 4:35-41). Jesus rebuked the boisterous storm of the sea that buffeted the boat. You can silence storms of life by sternly rebuking them. If Jesus had not rebuked the storm, they probably might have been involved in a shipwreck. Rebuking life circumstances and difficulties would set you free from danger, and yawning jaws of death. Over the years, I have personally rebuked storms of life and seemingly impossible situations. Jesus rebuked the wind. Why must you not rebuke demons and principalities?

Furthermore, Jesus rebuked demons that tormented people. In Capernaum, Jesus rebuked a demon that spoke via a tormented descendant of Abraham in the synagogue. The demon spoke up believing Christ had come to decimate the demonic kingdom. Christ did not dine with those demons or play with them. He sternly rebuked the demon. Scriptures asserts, "Be quite, Jesus said sternly. Come out of him. The evil spirit shook the man violently and came out of him with a shriek" (Mark 1:25). Rebuking Satan via the medium of prayer is biblical and canonical. Do not give a foothold to Satan. Another aspect is that the demon spoke through a human agent. There are some people whose utterances depict that they are agents of Satan, and not messengers of God. Such people may not be confronted but you have the spiritual missiles to rebuke their satanic auditory pronouncements. A person possessed by a demon of violence, assaults his victims either verbally or physically. People who are under the influence of demon of violence are combatants, insulting, abusing, bullying, bias, condescending and discriminatory. Another passage that exhaustively explains the power and authority that Jesus and disciples exercised over demons is Luke 10: 17-20. The demon of violence harasses its victim. We have sexual harassment, physical harassment, mental harassment, psychological harassment, emotional harassment, political harassment, social harassment, and verbal harassment. Demons harass their victims. You are imbued with the authority of Jesus to rebuke every demon that harasses you. You have the power of God to silence every demonic personality who harasses you. Jesus sternly rebuked the demon. Do not play with demons. Rebuke them.

# CHAPTER 8

## CULTIVATE THE HABIT OF PRAISING GOD

Praise in the Jewish and Christian communities is fulfilling one's duty to the supreme commander of the Universe. It was in consonance with this that King David declared that God was more delighted to receive praise from the people of the royal priesthood than sacrifice. "I will praise God's name in song and glorify him with thanks giving. This will please the LORD more than an ox, more than a bull with its horns and hoofs." (Psalm 69:30-31). Thus, the psalmist in Psalm 22:3 declares that the holy God is enthroned on the praises of Israel. That connotes the praises of the Christian forms unshakable platform for God to assume his reign over the entire creation.

Praise constitutes an armory of God that is capable of vanquishing the enemies of God. This is clearly indicated in Psalm 149: 6, "May the praise of God be their mouths, and doubled edged swords in their hands, to inflict vengeance on the nations." Even though the monarchy had been long vanquished, the weapon of praise was still available to be used to annihilate their enemies. There were certain times that the Psalmist had to summon his own soul to praise the Lord, by so doing they enjoined God to join them so that they could exude manifold praises to him. Praise is the watershed by which the Book of Psalms is carved out. The doxologies, which summarize the Psalms, bear incredible testimony to this analogy. Psalms 41:13;

72:18-19; 89:52; 106:48-50 are the pedestals that underscore the structure of the Book. This brings the reader to differentiate between **declarative praise** and **descriptive praise**. **Declarative** praise involves generic language such as "Praise the Lord" (Hebrew Hallelu= praise [imperative] +yah, the abridged form of Yahweh or LORD. This does not give the reasons praising the LORD. **Descriptive praise** on the other hand gives a detailed explanation of reasons why we must praise the LORD. Psalm 113 for example is an amalgamation of both declarative Psalm and a descriptive Psalm transiting from declarative praise to descriptive genre.[65]

## UNDERSTANDING PRAISE PALMS

Creation of God is a centerpiece of the Book of Psalms. Psalm 148: 5-6 is a typical example of the psalmist beckoning to the moons, stars, sun, and waters to praise the LORD. "For he commanded and they were created." Here, the verb create is the same verb used in Genesis 1.1. Even though the word "command" is not used in Genesis 1:1, the focal point here is that it was the word of God that brought creation into existence. Psalm 33:6, declares, "By the word of the LORD were the heavens made." Psalm 147: 4 is an evidence of God bringing creation into existence by his deed. God also created the universe by his understanding. Psalm 3:19; "By wisdom the LORD laid the earth's foundations and by his understanding he set the heavens in place." According to the writer, "wisdom" and "understanding" are used interchangeably in this context.

Psalm 103 is an epitome of praise. The psalmist is praising God for blessing us (1-5), praise God for blessing our nations (verses 6-14), praising God for present and everlasting providence (Verses 15-18), and a call on all to praise God (verses 19-22). It is one of the most beautiful and lovely Psalms. It is believed that it is evangelical in tone and thought. The psalmist in no doubt had emerged from

[65] C. Hassell Bullock, *Encountering the Book of Psalms*, (Grand Rapids, Michigan: Baker Academic, 2001), 152-158

doldrums into light; from complaint and supplication into praise and thanksgiving. It sets off with personal praise and climaxes with an inviting universal praise. It opens and closes with the same measure, an inclusio that defines the whole as praising thanks. The Psalm is a liturgical of all that the Lord has done for the psalmist and the universe as a whole. Thus the body of the Psalm is recollecting, remembering, and reminding. The remembering praise is divided into four parts. Each prominently features the steadfast love of God and the compassion of God as indicated in verses 4, 8, 11, 13, and 17. The psalm names the steadfast love (hesed) as the attribute of God expressed in all the lord's dealings and ways.

From verse 1-5 there is copious evidence that the psalmist is praising God in the first five verses for personal blessing. He blesses the name of the Lord. The psalmist is calling for real self, his whole self, and his highest self to respond to the blessings of the Lord with praise and gratitude. He praises God for his many benefits, including forgiveness of sin. He also acknowledges God for ransoming him from destruction. He acknowledges God for bestowing good things upon him. We need to acknowledge God for the many things that he has done for us. We have received so many blessings from the Lord as individuals as well as a community of believers. The Lord expects us to praise him, to extol him and venerate him. Verses 6-14 on the contrary dilate on the judgment of God. God brings right judgment and correction when the situation seems to be bad. God is described as being righteous, just, and true. Our God is true Lord who executes right acts for those who fear him. Being a merciful God, He causes us to know his ways as he did to Moses. In addition, because God is gracious he forgives us our sins, slow to get angry with us. God is not impulsive acting prematurely in dealing with our sins. He would not always strive with us but he bestows upon us his loving kindness. If the Lord had dealt with us according to our iniquities, we would not have survived. The Lord pities them that fear him.

## Praise God for present and everlasting providence

In the same Psalm 103 Verses 15-22, the psalmist cultivates the habit of praising God. Although the life of man is very frail and transient, God's loving kindness towards his chosen ones are from everlasting to everlasting. The loving kindness and righteousness can be passed on from one generation to the other. This can only be achieved by a continuous love and keeping the covenant of God. To live by the precepts of God is to do them. God expects us to abide by his covenant throughout our lives. He also expects us to teach them to our children who will in tend pass them unto their children. Having recognized the sovereignty of God over every creature, the psalmist calls on the angels, ministers of God, and all who fear Him to praise him. He calls upon the hosts of God that is the armies of Israel, the heavenly personages such as the moon, stars, and the sun to praise the Lord. He also calls on all who are the doers of God' word to praise him. We as children of God must always praise God for what he is and for the mighty works he done in his creation.

We must be aware that this Psalm contains praise for personal blessings, and indicates that God is forgiving. He lifts up and completely removes the burden of sin. It also contains expressions of praise for national blessings. We must cultivate the habit of praising God for our personal and national blessings. God continuous to execute right acts for those who fear him and obey his decrees. We must also know that He forgives and removes the burden of sin from us. God also heals, redeems, crowns, and satisfies us with good things.

## Cultivate the Habit of Thanking God

Scholars categorize the Psalms of thanksgiving into forms. Among many is the intention to worship. An outstanding example is Psalm 30: 1 "I will exalt you, O LORD for you lifted me out of depths and did not let my enemies gloat over me." David in this psalm states his intention to worship the LORD, which emanates from his heart of gratitude that the Lord had delivered him from the hands of his enemies.[66] The Psalm of Thanksgiving usually has a component of crisis report. An archetypal example is found in Psalm 52:1-7, where the psalms showers thanksgiving to God for delivering him from deceitful and arrogant personalities. The form of deliverance in the Psalms of Thanksgiving cannot be swept under the carpet. God's powerful deliverance from the Psalmist's crisis is the turn of events that really sets him in the direction of praise. The form of conclusion of the psalm of praise may assume a position of the Psalmist vowing to praise God or make a sacrifice to God.

The lexical item generally employed in literary analysis of Thanksgiving Psalms includes the form of the verb "to thank" (Hebrew yadah), or the noun form "thanks" or "thanksgiving" (todah). It must be pointed out that not all thanksgiving Psalms make use of these terms. Masterpieces of psalms, which do not use these terms, are psalms 31, 66, and 120. They do not use any form of the root ydh. Making allusions to Leopold Sabourin, the writer states, "and the psalms of thanksgiving are the final act in a human drama." He further states, "It is the destination of the human heart as it moves from complaint to trust to thanksgiving."[67] The contents of thanksgiving psalms are proliferated with the crisis in metaphors. For instance, "He lifted me out of the slimy pit, out of the mud and mire; he set my feet on a rock and gave me a firm place to stand," (Psalm 40:2). There are also a myriad of instances where the contents of thanksgiving psalms are interwoven with laments and a few graphic metaphors roped in to magnify the description. Some of the hearts wrenching experiences that the psalmist dreaded most were illnesses, death, spiritual as well as emotional turbulences, hostility and condescension by friends as well as enemies, expulsion from home and the looming threat of war.

[66] Ibid.,158
[67] Ibid., 158-159

Furthermore, the community of Yahweh people also depended on some prominent Psalms for their very survival. Concerning the content of the community thanksgiving, Psalms scholars have identified two major aspects of the poems. The first is the report of the crisis, and the second is the acknowledgement that the crisis has receded, which is characterized by plural pronouns as an element of community psalm. A clear case of such rendition is psalm 65: 3, "When we were overwhelmed by sins, you forgave our transgressions" An address to Israel is another community thanksgiving statement. "If the LORD had not been on our side-let Israel say" (psalm 129:1). Psalm 118: 1-4 and 22-27 is an obvious indication of the community joining the individual in showering torrential thanks to the almighty God. Psalms 124, and 129, are called declarative Psalms of praise of the people. Scholars in trying to resolve the scantiness problem of thanksgiving psalms came out with six thanksgiving poems, which are 65, 66, 107, 118, 124, and 129.

## THEOLOGICAL IMPLICATIONS OF THE PSALMS OF THANKSGIVING

Delving into Theological implications of the Psalms of Thanksgiving C. Hassell Bullock states, "Gratitude is a spiritual virtue that opens the door of the soul to the world around us. It creates a centrifugal force that causes the individual to look away from the self to God and to fellow human beings."[68] The psalmist is so delighted and encouraged, and inspired by the mighty works of God in the lives of the Israelites believing that God is capable of salvaging him from bondages and spiritual doldrums. For that matter psalm 66: 5-12 expatiate on the mighty and wonderful works of God on the Red Sea. "He turned the Red Sea into dry land" (V 6).[69] Based on divine works for the nation of Israel, the individual was so confident and recounted what the Lord had done for him. Hence,

---

[68] Ibid., 154-158

[69] Ibid., 159

the psalms of thanksgiving form a wealth of spiritual reservoirs, containing Holy Scriptures, which offer us spiritual meals to burn off life's passions and to afford us the opportunities to live above reproach by avoiding ingratitude.[70]

## DIRECT YOUR PRAYER TO THE MIRACLE WORKER- JESUS CHRIST

Jesus in his ministry performed unfathomable miracles, thus it is expedient to direct your prayers to him only. The Transfiguration of Jesus and raising up a twelve-year-old girl were undeniable miracles that Jesus performed in his ministry. He accomplished his first miracle at a wedding in Cana, turning water into wine. Apart from the miraculous activity of changing water into wine, Jesus also healed several people, ranging from the blind, the lamed, and the crippled. Even though leprosy individuals suffered as much as any other people suffering from diverse kinds of diseases, they suffered too much pain not from the disease, but from the pain of rejection imposed on them by the community and the society. The ostracized and sick were restored to health.

Jesus bestowed words of integrity and faith on some of the recipients of healing. For instance, Jesus commended the paralytic who was given access to Jesus through the roof. When Jesus saw the faith of the paralytic friends, he said, "Take heart, son: your sins are forgiven." Outstanding faith never failed to impress Jesus. Jesus is the master physician, for that matter, he never met a health problem he could not solve, a birth defect he could not reverse, and an evil spirit he could not exorcise. Jesus also multiplied five loaves of bread and two fishes to feed the five thousand people in a wilderness. The story of Lazarus enshrined in John 11 is heart wrenching for his sisters Martha and Mary but revealing, comforting and messianic focused in the end. Martha was crying, and Mary was also crying but Jesus moved with tears, "deeply moved in spirit and troubled",

[70] Ibid.,159-163

raised up Lazarus from the dead after he was buried for four days. In Jesus, what seems to be dead and rotten will be resurrected. What appeared to have been lost will be recovered. We were condemned to destruction but in Jesus, we found our salvation. With God all things are possible. You will not die of **cardiovascular disease.** You will not perish of **coronary disease,** nor will you not die of **gastric byp ass condition,** you will not perish from **diabetics, or high cholesterol.** You are destined to receive a miracle from the Lord Jesus, the master physician. That stomach ulcer or intestinal problems will not kill you.

## PERSISTENT PRAYER IN LUKE 18:1-8

Jesus having lived a prayerful lifestyle uses parables to instruct believers to constantly be on their knees seeking the face of God and not to give up even when it seems God is far away from us. Luke 18:1-8 therefore is one of such tantalizing, heartwarming, spiritually energizing, and encouraging parables used by Jesus to exhort all his disciples to persist in prayer until the coming Kingdom is established. The phrase *"you ought always to pray"* in verse, one indicates ceaseless bending of the knee with petitions to the almighty, but an attitude of unbroken fellowship with God. St. Augustine notes, *"There is another interior prayer without intermission, and that is the longing of the heart".* It is in support of this that Paul categorically states in 1 Thes. 5:17 that we should endeavor to pray without ceasing. According to Raymond E. Brown, the parable of the unjust judge in (18:1-8) is designed to encourage the disciples by a fortiori principle. If continued petitioning persuades a very amoral judge, God who bestows his loving kindness on children at all times, vindicate the chosen ones if they prevail in persistent, and confident prayer. In Mark 8:22-26, even Jesus had to lay his hands on the blind man twice before he could be totally healed. Paul also prayed three times for a particular thorn in his side to be taken away (2 Cor.12:18). In view of this, the parable sets a tone for the elect to be persistent in seeking the face of God until their prayers are answered. According to Richard and Holly Lang., the word *"persistent"* when translated from Greek means *"continual persistence and being given your rights or your vindication"*. Moreover, the word *"necessary has to do with an essential duty or obligation"*. That means we are obliged to pray. It is necessary for us to pray.

## ATTITUDE OF THE WIDOW AND THE UNJUST JUDGE

If the judge had no regard for men how much less regard would he have for a mere widow? Widows were looked down upon and had no place in society and very often, they had little or no rights. The recalcitrant behavior of the judge indicates that he is hard-boiled and unyielding. He is tough, hard-bitten, and self-centered. He epitomizes egoistic personalities of his time and in the 21$^{st}$ century communities and societies. Just as the judge was not worthy of emulation, so are evil minded and criminal personalities who blatantly refuse to bestow justice on the righteous in our contemporary societies. However, this widow knew her rights and she had the boldness to pursue her rights. The Greek Language uses the imperative form of the verb, meaning the woman ordered the judge to bestow upon her, her rights. In verses 6, 7, and 8 Jesus contrasted the unrighteous judge's hearing the window's plea with God hearing the prayer of the elect. Therefore, the unjust judge stands for God in the analogy. This analogy is used not to show similarity but to point out the contrast. It is the same as when Jesus' own coming is compared to the coming of a thief in the night (Thess. 5:2). The point of comparison here is not to indicate that Jesus is a die-hard thief who robs people while they are asleep but that his coming will be sudden and unexpected. Similarly, the point of comparison between God and the judge is not to say God is insensitive, proud, and boastful but that he responds with help to those who cry to him day and night. In verse 7, Jesus draws out the lesson, which intends *"Always pray and don't lose heart "and God not avenge his own elect who cry day and night to Him, though he bears long with them"*. This verse indicates that if saints cry to God day and night and if they always pray and do not lose heart, they will not be left in judgment. If they endure in faith and love, God will vindicate them when the son of man comes. Believers are exhorted to pray and should not lose heart because God will never leave us in mid-stream at the time we need him most.

Additionally, the last verse of the text, Luke 18:8; refers to the Second Coming of Christ. *"I tell you, he will vindicate them speedily. Nevertheless, when the son of man comes, will he find faith on earth?"* Most scholars have indicated that we should read it as a conclusion to the section on the coming of the Kingdom just before it, Luke 17:20-37. In the above text, Jesus describes the characteristics of the last days leading to the return of the Messiah. There is no doubt that he compares the coming of the son of man to the flood in Noah's days and the decimation of Sodom and Gomorrah due to their promiscuous, ungodly and inhospitable behavior. He makes it very clear that the days preceding his return will be like those ungodly days before God poured his wrath on the people. John Piper argues that Luke 18:1-8 is part of this end-time teaching. It closes in verse 8 with a question, *"when the son of man comes will he find faith on earth?"* will the warnings of Jesus to remember lot's wife, to keep the heart fixed on Christ and not love the world be found in us? Will Christ find all saints trusting in his word and living a godly lifestyle? If we continue to cry to God in our relationship with him, when Christ returns, we shall reign with him in his everlasting kingdom.

Prominently, there is no doubt that the widow who knew her rights was not hesitant in coming, speaking, and asking continually. She was willing to bring her demands to the judge. Even though it took her some time before the judge granted her what she really deserved, she did not lose heart. This implies that we should also know our rights in the word of God and we should not hesitate to come and speak continually to God. At the right time, he will answer and relief us of all pain. Even though the widow had a persecutor, someone who was harassing her, plaguing her, and making life extremely difficult for her she found a way out. She brought her demand to the judge, who even though was so amoral, granted her,

her demand at last. We are entreated to pray always and not to lose heart. For, prayer always stirs the heart of God and always moves God to act. Even though it sometimes takes time for our requests to be granted to us, we should persevere in prayer. For the father knows, and because he is the father he knows that it is not yet time to answer in that particular way. Wesley said, *"God does not immediately put an end, either to the wrongs of the wicked or the sufferings of good men"*. Do not resort to psyche consultation, or to traditional gods for antidotes. The key to success is Christocentric prayer.

# CHAPTER 9

## PRAYER AND SPIRITUAL MATURITY

Different people have defined spiritual maturity in diverse ways. Each group of people has their own school of thought concerning spiritual maturity. For one group of people, spiritual maturity means having a firm grip on the Bible. That is knowing biblical stories and having the aptitude to quote innumerable verses. Consequently, the more a person knows the Bible, the more he is spiritually mature. To some, spiritual maturity means being able to praise and worship God. For them, once such a person is constantly engaged in this aspect of worship it indicates that he or she spiritually mature. Whilst another school of thought postulates that spiritual maturity is enshrined in piety. The more intimate relationship one has with God, the more mature he or she is.

For another group of people, true spiritual maturity is made apparent in social action. This is made clear in serious involvement with the poor, the outcast, the downtrodden and the despaired and forsaken. They claim that Jesus came for these people, and if one fulfills this obligation then one is spiritually mature. To still others, spiritual maturity means experiencing the fullness of the spirit and exercising the gifts of the Holy Spirit in increasing measure.[71] Some

---

[71] Perry Downs, *Teaching for Spiritual Growth* (Michigan: Zondervan 1994), 17.

of these people stress that tongue speaking is a sign of spiritual maturity. At best, they can be described as Christian fundamentalists. Hence, it is obvious that Christian disagree on what it means to be spiritually mature. However, let us consider what the bible says about spiritual maturity.

The Bible has used a multiplicity of expressions and images to illustrate spiritual maturity. In 2 Cor 9: 13, the term *proved* is used while Eph 4: 13, the term *mature* is used, *holy* in 1 Thess 4:3, and *complete* in James 1: 4. In the last passage, the writer educates that mature Christians are those who endure trials without seeking a quick deliverance so that the full work may be done. Accordingly, a mature Christian does not grow weary and seek premature relief. Prayer is one of the required modalities that makes the believer to endure severe trials. He must endure to the end so that he might be fully developed and mature in grace. Without ceaseless petition, supplication, defensive and offensive maneuvers against Satan, resisting temptation and enduring trials would be extremely difficult. *Wanting nothing* used in the verse means he must be strong, being grounded and settled in faith[72]. All these passages refer to the concept of spiritual maturity. Metaphors, such as Christ *dwelling* in believers in Eph3: 17, *abiding* or *remaining* in Christ in John 15: 5 and believers *walking in Jesus* as illustrated in1 John 2:6 also describe the concept of spiritual maturity. Since no single definition has been given, a theological definition must be offered to sum up biblical data in a momentous way. According to Perry Downs, the concept of *faith and belief* can be used to determine spiritual maturity. He underscores the fact that the term faith is used in a number of ways to express what God requires from his people and is useful in recounting what spiritual maturity is.[73]

---

[72] Henry T. Mahan, *Bible Class Commentary, Hebrews and James* (England: Evangelical Press, 1984), 84.
[73] Perry Downs, *Teaching for Spiritual Growth* (Michigan: Zondervan, 1994), 17.

# Cognitive, Relational, Volitional Faith and Spiritual Maturity

Perry downs underscores the fact that faith must be cognitive which he describes as intellectual (noticia). This statement educates that faith means believing that certain things are true. There is a content to believe which must be specific. Consequently, in 1 Thess 4:14, Paul categorically states that we believe that Jesus Christ died and rose again. Faith supersedes mere hope, thus the experience of faith is more important that it is content. In view of this having, knowledge of God and knowledge of the word of God is paramount in spiritual maturity. He states emphatically, *"It is impossible to be spiritually mature and yet be ignorant of the truths of God's word. Spiritual maturity is contingent upon knowing what God has said."* In summary, whoever claims to be spiritually mature must have deep knowledge about God and his word. Knowledge of God and His word are a foundation stone for spiritual maturity.

Another area that cannot be swept under the carpet when it comes to spiritual maturity is the ability to have relational faith. This is described as assensus. In other words, true faith causes us to assent to the truthfulness of our object of faith and to have our hearts controlled. This belief transcends our intellectual aspects of belief but causes us to be totally committed to the object of our faith. Thus the mature believer will have a hear that loves God. This is because God is love and a mature Christian must cultivate the habit of loving God and his neighbor.

A mature Christian must also have a volitional faith in God. This causes people to convert their belief into action. In John 14: 15, Jesus declares, "if you love me you will do what I command." A mature Christian knows that he is not justified by faith that stands alone. Faith must be accompanied by good deeds. Ephesians 2: 10 states in affirmative terms that, *"For we are God's workship, created in Christ Jesus to do good works, which God preached in advance for us."* This educates that maturity is made manifest in our good works and not by faith alone. Hence, true maturity affects the will causing the person to have an ardent desire to please God in producing good fruits. The fruits he bears are made manifest to the Christian world and to the unbelieving world.

## Holiness of God and Spiritual Maturity

The idea of the holiness of God is central to biblical teaching that is said of God. "Holy is His name." His name is holy because he is holy. There can be no more worship, no spiritual growth, and no true obedience without it. God has declared, "Be holy, for I am holy."[74] The Hebrew word for "to be holy," *quadesh,* is derived from the root *qad* meaning to cut or separate. This is applied primarily to God. The Greek words *hagiazo and hagios* in the New Testament also convey the same meaning. The ethical holiness of God is defined as that perfection of God, in virtue of which He eternally wills and maintains His own moral excellence, abhors sin, and demands purity in His moral creatures[75]. That means that God demands purity or holiness form all Christians. The holiness of God will make us realize our own sinfulness and may want to live morally upright lifestyles. Thus, a person who is spiritually mature, asks God to afford him the privilege to live for him daily in the purity of God.

I remember when we were growing up, we cultivated the habit of fasting and praying and any time we fasted, we were able to subdue all sins including sexual temptations. This made us spiritual valiant personalities for several years. There were certain times, I did not know what sin to confess to God. I was so immaculate in my lifestyle that I could be associated with the word holiness. Because of our standing with God, any time we prayed for demon-possessed people they were slain and the spirits exorcised. Those who were sick were restored to good health. We experienced an upsurge in our spiritual

---

[74] Sproul R.C, *The Holiness of God,* (Wheaton, Illinois: Tyndale House, 1985) 24-25.

[75] Louis Berkhof, *Systematic Theology* (Grand Rapids, Michiga: William B. Eermanns, 1996), 73-74.

journey with the Lord. Prayer helps you to succeed as a believer. Do you want to be holy and righteous in your deeds? Then pray, because prayer is the **key** to unfathomable breakthroughs in your life.

## CONSEQUENTIALIST AND EGOIST THEORIES

Furthermore, prayer coupled with the word of God will fortify you to make the right **ethical choices.** Prayer, the word of God and knowledge of God will help you determine whether you are a **consequentialist or not.** According to Hollinger, the consequentialist believes that the standard for right and wrong of any action wholly depends on the results. For example, stealing in itself is not wrong but the consequences that arise because of stealing may cause it to be morally unwarranted. One tells the truth not because he is obligated to do so, but because in most cases, telling the truth produces the best results. Thus, consequences are the underpinning of ethics. Scripture clearly states[76], "You shall not steal" (Ex. 20:15). Jesus asserts, "Do not murder, do not commit adultery, **do not steal**, do not give false testimony" (Mt. 19:18). Homogeneously, Paul penning to the Ephesians states, " **He who has been stealing must steal no longer, but must work, doing something useful with his own hands, that he may have something to share with those in need" (Eph. 4:28).**

In relation to this, is ethical egoism. Ethical egoists believe ethics are firmly embedded in results but the ultimate goal is the maximum gratification or good that will be accrued to the individual is what matters. The weakness of ethical egoism is that it is a self-centered theory. One will only engage in action that would satisfy him alone. Scriptures teach that we have to love our neighbors as ourselves. Christians must consider other people's welfare. In Phil 2:4, *"each of you should look not only to your own interests, but also to the interests of others."* Thus, prayer, sound education, the fear of God coupled with the word of God will energize you to have compassion for others.

---

[76] Dennis P. Hollinger, *Choosing the Good: Christian Ethics in a Complex World* (Grand Rapids, Michigan: Baker Academics, 2002), 27-28.

## Utilitarianism

Christocentric prayer helps you to eschew utilitarian ethical point of view. Proponents and adherents of utilitarianism hold the school of thought that moral good is rooted in consequences. An action is described as morally good if the moral consequences relate to the greatest number of people.[77] Thus, the greatest good for the greatest number of people is the utilitarian mantra. For example, if executing a criminal resulted in the greatest amount of pleasure for the greatest number of people then, it is a moral good and vice versa. This philosophical undertone was further developed by British Jeremy Bentham (1748- 1832) and John Stuart. Jeremy believed that nature has offered humankind two important sovereign masters, pain and pleasure. It is to them a lone that we are accountable to. One should always work had to maximize abnormal pleasure and minimize pain. John Stuart carried this idea further by eliminating God from the life of human kind. The rule therefore is that greatest good is the mantra. One has to tell the truth not because truth is inherently good but truth brings pleasure to a majority of people.

This is contrary to Christian worldview. This theory teaches the principle of the end justifies the means. Some means may not be morally good. For instance in 1798 Malthus suggested that people should die through famine, wars and diseases in order to curb population growth. For Christians, this is awful because the Bible teaches the sanctity of life. Man is created in the image of God. Thus, certain issues in Christianity are worthy of pursuit not because they bring the greatest good but because they are the imperatives from God. For example, the Bible says thou shall not kill, steal, murder or commit adultery. These should not be committed not because they bring the least satisfaction to the greatest number of people but God demands of them. Honesty, sincerity, truth and hard work are also imperatives from the supreme God. We as Christian must always execute righteousness and justice because God requires us of them and not because they bring the greatest good.

---

[77] Ibid., 31-35

# Deontological ethics

Unvaryingly, prayer, the word of God and theological Education will energize you to approach deontological ethics in the 21ˢᵗ Century universal Church with Christian World View. This approach teaches that moral actions are inherently wrong or right and devoid of reliance on outcomes or extrinsic dynamics. This is an ethic, which views rights, duties and may come from a number of sources such as religion, reason and wisdom. These emanate from all sources of human endeavors and experiences. Socrates and Emmanuel Kant were ardent proponents of deontological ethics.[78]

Even though it necessary for Christians to orchestrate right actions, it should not be the foundation of our ethical principles. Our foundation must be anchored in the word of God, which reveals the will of God to us. The Decalogue may be a sure biblical command for us, but they are not our moral foundation. We are saved by grace and not by works. Our moral character must not be based only on deontological ethics alone but must be anchored in the redeeming quality of God through the revelation of God, Knowing that Christ is the author and finisher of our faith. We are justified by faith and not by works.

# Character/ virtue ethics

Since the beginning of creation, men and women of God have often struggled with **Character/virtue ethics.** Hollinger examines the sub topics consequentialism and character. If for example, a committed Christian husband has been faithful to his spouse for 30 years but happens to commit adultery due to circumstances beyond his control, the consequentialist will judge him based on his action. The character of virtue ethicist will argue that since it is not his behavior over this period, he should not be blamed or judged. Thus,

---

[78] Ibid., 37-39

he defines character as *"the inner and distinctive core of a person from which moral discernment, decisions, and actions spring. It is an enduring configuration of the intensions, feelings, dispositions, and perceptions of any particular self."* In view of this, habits that are desirable are termed virtues and the undesirable ones are known as vices. In conformity with Biblical principles which deal with the heart. Actions spring directly from the heart will be a good foundation for character ethics. Aristotle and Carol Gilligan and Stanley Hauer were ardent proponents of character/ virtue paradigm.

Positive aspects of this approach are the heart since the Bible shows that what is in our heart determines our behavior. The heart occurs more than hundred times in the English Bible. The Old Testament *shama* clearly affirms character in the classic text of the Deuteronomy 6:4-7. Jesus in his teachings emphasized that external teachings propounded by the teachers of the law were insignificant concerning matters such as adultery, which comes from within the inner core of man- the heart. Jesus declares, *"What comes out of a man is what makes him unclean. For from within, out of men's hearts, come evil thoughts, sexual immorality, theft, murder, adultery, greed, malice, deceit, lewdness, envy, slanders, arrogance, and folly. All these evils come from inside and make a man unclean."* On April 14, 2013, Colan Nolan of NBC interviewed the mayor of Los Angeles. He asked the mayor (Antonio Villaragoza) to name one **single mistake that made him unpopular. He conceded that the CEO recommendation that led to laying off of workers caused him so much pain and regret.** A public officer or a CEO who believes in prayer and prays will avoid character ethics.

## CHRISTIAN WORLDVIEW FOUNDATION FOR ETHICS

Pertaining to *Christian worldview Foundation for Ethics*, Denis Hollinger defines worldview as *"the way we put our world together. It embodies our sense of God or transcendence, our understanding of human nature, and our beliefs about what is wrong within the world and how to fix that wrong, and our perceptions about where history is headed.[79]"*

Peter singer's ethical principles state that humans are not different from animals and thus do not have greater moral importance. For instance, he argues that it is better to terminate the life of a handicapped baby than to kill a happy cat. He argues that there is nothing dignified and worthy in humans because there is nothing in the cosmic world that is beyond humans to bestow dignity, respect and worth upon man. Since most worldviews deny the role of God in their world of behavior, the Christian worldview is rooted in the triune God. God is the foundation and ground of Christian ethics. Hence, our understanding of moral good, right, justice, mercy and love emanate from God's actions and nature. He also gives the Christian the ability to live out his worldview in the full view of the world.

## MOTIFS FOR MAKING ETHICAL DECISION

Concerning Christian motifs for making ethical decisions, he outlines three important watersheds of Christian moral principles, which include deliberative, prescriptive and relational motifs.

## DELIBERATIVE MOTIF

Deliberative motif underscores the fact that reason is equated to divine revelation for making ethical decisions. This approach educates that reason can be a moral guide because he has planted in the conscious of man a natural law that is comprehensible to all.[80] This is st. Aquinas and the Roman Catholic Tradition. Aquinas believed that man could be guided by reason because God is supreme, and is pure in reason. Since we are made in the image of God, we

---

[79] Ibid., 61
[80] Ibid., 128

are able to use reason to make ethical decisions. St. Thomas Aquinas law of reason became the moral fiber in Catholicism as far as moral theology was concerned.[81] This approach has constructive aspects. In the first place, God affirms that the knowledge of God can be discerned through nature. Paul argues in Roman chapter one that the unrighteous have no excuse whatsoever, for the knowledge of God has been revealed to them through nature. In Christian Education, this is described as general revelation of God. Hence, to some extent this approach is acceptable in Christian worldview. It is also positive in the sense that humans universally accept that some vices and socially unacceptable behaviors such as adultery, murder, theft, lying, cheating and injustice are universally condemned as violations of the rights of men and women.[82]

It has its own weaknesses and challenges as far making morally acceptable decisions are concerned. There is too much over dependence of rationality as a yardstick for making ethical decisions. The proponents of this approach have failed to appreciate the fallen nature of man. Overestimation of this approach without having relation with God may lead to ethical disaster. It also divorces ethics from the broader worldview foundations

## PRESCRIPTIVE MOTIF

The prescriptive motif on the other hand postulates rules, principles, or moral actions that are resultant from divine revelation. One must always apply scripture in every ethical situation to discern the will of God. John Calvin, Carl. F.H.Henry and Richard Mouw had affinities to this approach. It is very positive because it gives preeminence to the authority of scripture. It helps the average Christian to understand the design of God. Informed decision is based on application of the inspired word of God.[83]

---

[81]  Ibid.,129
[82]  Ibid., 128
[83]  Ibid.,135-137

# Relational motif

Relational motif on the other hand offers a general orientation for moral life. Augustine, Martin Luther, Jonathan Edwards have long been associated with this approach. *"For Augustine, moral action was primarily a result of the will and what one loves; for Luther, it was a spontaneous overflow of justifying faith; and for Edwards, it was a benevolent propensity of heart to in general, and a temper or disposition to love God supremely."* [84]Its main weakness is that it is subjective and it is over dependence on community as the source of moral direction. Its positive dimensions are that decisions are shaped by a dynamic encounter with God. It also postulates that a Christian ethics must be theological.[85]

# Bible in ethical decisions

Acceptable ethical decisions are anchored in scripture. Over the centuries, most Christians have resorted to the Bible to find workable solutions to moral dilemmas. The Bible, should not be regarded as a book of moral codes or ethics textbook. Even though it is not wrong to do so, the Bible is more than a book of moral codes because there are some ethical issues that are not enshrined in the Bible. The bible is not also a foundational document to solve problems as some see it, but a true authority of God, the true word of God.[86] The Bible does not address many contemporary issues but to address them, scriptures must be used in such a manner that even though they are not directly mentioned in the Bible, they can be used in a broader perspective focusing on the Bible. Empirical judgments in ethical decisions such as wars, environmental ethics, poverty and economic justice have been critically examined.[87]

---

[84]  Ibid., 141-142
[85]  141-142
[86]  Ibid., 149
[87]  Ibid., 150-155

There is a school of thought that educates that Christ is against culture. Tertullian even though highly lettered rejected philosophy, arts and the attendance of amphitheater shows of his day. Another group of people who are ardent adherents to this school of thought were the Anabaptists.[88]

Some however taught that Christ came for the cultures of the people and not to reject it outright. Adherents teach that there is no tension between the best of culture and the heart of Christian thought and values. For them, both are expressions of God's goodness. Peter Abeland, cultural Protestantism and contemporary expressions are advocates of liberal Christianity, which, I believe must be avoided.[89]

On the other hand, clement of Alexandria, and Thomas Aquinas taught that Christ is above culture while John Calvin taught that Christ is the transformer of culture. This school of thought educates that man and his culture are engrossed in sin but something can be done to convert the social order into a much loved religious model.[90]

---

[88]  Ibid., 191-199
[89]  Ibid.,191-200
[90]  Ibid.,191-202

# CHAPTER 10

## PRAYER AND HEART DISEASE STATISTICS

According to *center for Disease and Prevention*, In 2008, over 616,000 people died of heart disease. It also affirms that In 2008, heart disease caused almost 25% of deaths—almost one in every four—in the United States.[91] Furthermore, according to CBS morning news anchored by Charlie Rose, Oneil, and King on February 19, 2014, 1 out of four Americans die of heart disease. The Center for Disease Control and prevention, *"Heart disease is the leading cause of death for both men and women. More than half of the deaths due to heart disease in 2008 were in men. The studies also dilates that Coronary heart disease is the most common type of heart disease. In 2008, 405,309 people died from coronary heart disease. Every year about 785,000 Americans have a first coronary attack. Another 470,000 who have already had one or more coronary attacks have another attack. In 2010, coronary heart disease alone was projected to cost the United States $108.9 billion. This total includes the cost of health care services, medications, and lost productivity."[92].*

---

[91] https://www.cardiosmart.org/Heart-Basics/CVD-Stats (Accessed on February 9, 2014), P.1

[92] https://www.cardiosmart.org/Heart-Basics/CVD-Stats (Accessed on February 9, 2014), P.1

## WOMEN AND HEART DISEASE

*"Furthermore, according to Center for Disease Control and Prevention, "more than 42 million women are currently living with some form of cardiovascular disease. More than 8 million women have a history of heart attack and/or angina. Five and a half million women will suffer angina. Heart disease is the leading cause of death of American women, killing more than a third of them. 35.3% of deaths in American women over the age of 20, or more than 432,000, are caused by cardiovascular disease each year. More than 200,000 women die each year from heart attacks- five times as many women as breast cancer. More than 159,000 women die each year of congestive heart failure, accounting for 56.3% of all heart failure deaths. 48% of adult women have a total cholesterol of at least 200mg/dL. 50% of Caucasian women, 64% of African-American women, 60% of Hispanic women, and 53% of Asian/Pacific Islander women are sedentary and get no leisure time physical activity. 58% of Caucasian women, 80% of African-American women, and 74% Hispanic-American women are overweight or obese. Women with diabetes are 2.5 times more likely to have heart attacks. More women than men die of heart disease each year. 23% of women and 18% of men will die within one year of a first recognized heart attack; 22-32% of women and 15-27% of men heart attack survivors will die within five years. 12-25% of women and 7-22% of men heart attack survivors will be diagnosed with heart failure within five years. Women are less likely than men to receive appropriate treatment after a heart attack.Women comprise only 27% of participants in all heart-related research studies.Percent of women 18 years and over who met the 2008 federal physical activity guidelines for aerobic activity through leisure-time aerobic activity: 44.6% Percent of women 18 years and over who currently smoke: 16.5%. Percent of women 18 years and over who had 5 or more drinks in 1 day at least once in the past year: 13.6%."*[93] Percent of women 20

---

[93] https://www.cardiosmart.org/Heart-Basics/CVD-Stats (Accessed on February 9, 2014), P.2

years and over who are obese: 35.9% (2007-2010). Percent of women 20 years and over with hypertension: 32.8% (2007-2010)".[94]

## OVERWEIGHT/OBESITY

"The statistics has proven that adults aged 20 years and over constituted 35.9% obesity rate in (2009-2010). The same age group recorded 33.3% as overweight within the same period. Children aged 12-19 years were observed to be obese with a record of 18.4% in 2009-2010. Children aged 6-11 years were diagnosed with obesity at a percent of 18.0 in 2009-2010. Percent of children aged 2-5 years who were obese constituted 12.1% in (2009-2010). In 2008, medical costs associated with obesity were estimated at $147 billion; the medical costs for people who suffered from obesity were $1,429 higher than those of normal weight. Non-Hispanic blacks have the highest age-adjusted rates of obesity (49.5%) compared with Mexican Americans (40.4%), all Hispanics (39.1%) and non-Hispanic whites (34.3%). Among non-Hispanic black and Mexican-American men, those with higher incomes are more likely to be obese than those with low income. Women whose income were higher were less likely to be obese than low-income women. May be due to easy access to medical treatment, gyms, and fitness clubs. There is no significant relationship between obesity and education among men. Among women, however, there is a trend—those with college degrees are less likely to be obese compared with less educated women."[95] "Over

[94] https://www.cardiosmart.org/Heart-Basics/CVD-Stats (Accessed on February 9, 2014), P.2. Reference to *Women Heart and Centers for Disease Control and Prevention.*

[95] https://www.cardiosmart.org/Heart-Basics/CVD-Stats (Accessed on February 9, 2014), P.2. Reference to *Women Heart and Centers for Disease Control and Prevention(Source: Centers for Disease Control and Prevention).*

all diabetes affected 25. 8 million people of all ages (8.3% of the U.S. Population) in 2010".[96]

## High Blood Pressure

According to Center for Disease Control and Prevention, about "1 in 3 U.S. adults—an estimated 68 million—has high blood pressure. High blood pressure is a major risk factor for heart disease, stroke, congestive heart failure, and kidney disease. High blood pressure was listed as a primary or contributing cause of death for more than 347,000 Americans in 2008. In 2010, high blood pressure was projected to cost the United States $93.5 billion in health care services, medications, and missed days of work. About 1 in 2 U.S. adults with high blood pressure has it under control. Almost 30% of American adults have prehypertension—blood pressure numbers that are higher than normal, but not yet in the high blood pressure range. Prehypertension raises your risk for high blood pressure."[97]

## High Cholesterol

"Approximately one in every six adults—16.3% of the U.S. adult population—has high total cholesterol.[1] The level defined as high total cholesterol is 240 mg/dL and above. People with high total cholesterol have approximately twice the risk of heart disease as people with optimal levels. A desirable level is lower than 200 mg/dL. For adult Americans, the average level is about 200 mg/dL, which is

---

[96] *Source: National Diabetes Information Clearinghouse (NDIC), National Institute of Diabetes and Digestive and Kidney Diseases (NIDDK), National Institutes of Health.*

[97] *Source: Centers for Disease Control and Prevention*

borderline high risk. More women than men have high cholesterol in the United States."[98]

Jesus has divine power to heal every disease. The Greek word for power is **dunamis** and the word for signs, wonders or miracles is **dunameis**. Phonologically, the two lexical items almost appear to be the same except the insertion of /e/ in **dunameis**. Peter demonstrating divine power, healed a cripple at the beautiful gate in Acts chapter 3:8. Even the shadows of Peter healed a great number of people suffering from diverse kinds of infirmities as the apostles preached Christ crucified in Judea (5: 15, 16). Jesus performed several miracles in his lifetime. Peter prayed and resurrected Tabitha (Acts 9: 36-42). Her name in Aramaic meant a "gazelle" and the Greek equivalent of this name is "Dorcas" whose connotation is the same. The people of Joppa were wailing, and weeping for the premature departure of their beloved Tabitha. The city was thrown into pandemonium because Tabitha was a good woman. She was beneficial to the community of believers. When peter got to the city of Joppa from Lydda, he fell to his knees in prayer, and then called the dead woman's name, her eyes opened and she sat up. Prayer resurrects the dead. You will be healed of diabetes, cardiovascular diseases, and High Blood pressure if you believe in the power of prayer.

As a healer, Jesus assigned much of his time healing the sick, setting people from spiritual and physical bondage. He exhibited indubitable authority and power in healing the sick and delivering the demon possessed (4: 23-25; 9:35; 14: 34 36; 15: 29-31; 21: 14). Principalities, demons, rulers of the dark world know who Jesus is. They know he is the one who will destroy them because he is the son of God and is holy. Wherever Jesus went, the evil spirits recognized him and yelled out to him, "You are the son of God" (3:11). He exercised authority over the storm by rebuking it. Even in the territory of the gentiles such as Gerasenes Jesus is recognized

---

[98] *Source: Centers for Disease Control and Prevention. Information on cardiovascular and other diseases was taken from Centers for Disease Control and Prevention website. Using the information, I employed the word of God as a means of spiritual healing and deliverance.*

as "the son of the most high God" (5:7). In the Jewish region, a woman who suffered from hemorrhage for 12 years received her healing. Jarus' daughter is raised from the dead, and Jesus feeds five thousand people with five loaves of bread and two fish in an isolated environment (6: 39-44). These and other many miraculous deeds of Jesus such as healing of diseases of diverse kinds, the people interrogating him of the source of his authority are recorded in the gospel of Mark. Believe in Jesus and pray and you will receive your miracle of healing. You are not destined to die of HIV/AIDS. You are not destined to die of heart attack or cardiac arrest. You are not ordained to die of diabetes or high Cholesterol. You are not designed to die of high blood pressure. You are not predestined to die of gastric bypass. You are not preordained to die from surgery. As legal citizen of the commonwealth of Israel, you have the right to demand your healing and deliverance from the Lord. Do not doubt the healing power of Jesus. Call on him and prevail in prayer for divine healing.

## JESUS PREVENTED ME FROM DYING OF HEART ATTACK

On June 29, 2010 I was hospitalized at Harbor UCLA for reasons best known to the doctors. I found myself amongst lunatics, and I knew that the enemy hard worked his way to possessing my destiny. I knew that I did not belong to that class. I was overdozed with destructive substances and drugs. On July 10, 2010 after breaking and having been forced to dance to Michael Jackson' music I suffered a heart attack. I knew something had to be done about it or I would die the next 30 seconds. My heart beat seized, I was choked and my trachea blocked completely. I prayed earlier on asking God to help me to survive premature death and be discharged from the hospital. When I realized I was almost gone to heaven prematurely, I walked to the Dr. Griffith and told her I was almost gone. She instructed a nurse by name Noah to attend to me. A pill was given to me immediately to swallow. Actually, I was seconds away from death but jesus intervened and gave me the wisdom to pray and to use another' patient's Bible for personal devotion. Prayer in the name of Jesus heals and saves.

On July 21, 2010, I was discharged from the hospital and had to live in a deplorable condition with some friends. Then, on August 10, 2010 after I took my medication, I suffered from another heart attack. I had nobody to support me. I had no friend or Frafra or Mamprusi, Dagomba, Ashanti, Ga, Ghanaian Or American to help me survive the days. My life had ebbed away and I felt this time around the enemy had succeeded. I was gasping for air, I was choked up once again. I had no cellphone to call 911, my friends were out of our deplorable abode. Once again, I prayed to God and walked to a nearby clinic. When I got to the clinic, they said it was not an emergency clinic and that I needed to be transported somewhere else. Miraculously, one woman spoke up and two Doctors showed up. One wanted me to be carried in an ambulance so that they could have the opportunity to kill me. However, a nurse was instructed to give me oxygen via a machine. I pulled it off because it nearly killed me. After a few minutes of treatment, I regained some little strength and vitality. I was led upstairs where Dr. Casillas treated me. He examined my heart thoroughly and made to go to the laboratory for diagnosis. I prayed and pleaded with Patrick, the laboratory technician not to infuse HIV virus into my system because that clinic is designated for HIV/AIDS treatment. Once again, I was delivered by Jesus.

# CONCLUSION

In conclusion, I must indicate that *Using prayer to unlock your 21st Century Destiny* is a masterpiece that unravels all the theological and Biblical wealth for research, personal devotion and spiritual enhancement. The Book has succinctly and academically illustrated the types of prayers enshrined in the Old Testament and their theological and Biblical importance to the nation of Israel as well as their significance to the 21st Century believer. There is copious evidence that the Pentateuch played a pivotal role in shaping the nation of Israel. The patriarchs were the first group of people to receive the Abrahamic covenant promises. Thus, the author is beckoning to all believers to emulate them in order to embrace the manifold blessings of the Lord. Pertaining to the historical Books, the author has unearthed to all readers that the narratives are loaded with spiritual as well as theological wealth needed for emulation. The fact that the author devoted a considerable amount of time elucidating the significance of the historical narratives is worthy of praise. Old Testament Kings such as Asa, Hezekiah, David, and Jehosaphat play an important role in this magnus opus. In addition, the author has also discussed the theological and biblical significance of the poetical Books for the nation of Israel and for the 21st century believers. They are worthy of praise, worthy of studying, and for personal devotion.

I must emphasize that *Using prayer to unlock your 21st Century Destiny* is a work of a genius and for that reason all Cardinals, Bishops, pastors, Seminarians, and biblical expositors must endeavor to imbibe the Book because it contains spiritual bouillabaisse needed for teaching, and preaching and for our personal spiritual impetus.

The Book has exhaustively explained all the major theological and biblical principles needed for academic research, preaching, and teaching the word of God through Jesus Christ who laid the biblical and Spiritual foundation for all believers to emulate. The salvation work of Jesus for humanity, his vicarious death, and resurrection cannot be glossed over. Apart from, Jesus laying a solid theological and spiritual structure for humanity, his apostles continued to preach the gospel starting the invincible New Church in Palestine as comprehensively explained in Acts of the Apostles. Portions of Acts of Apostles are excerpted to explain how Paul, Peter, Silas and a myriad of others used prayer to overcome seemingly impossible problems.

The authors has also penned so much on Church planting and Missionary activities in the Book. Paul and his compatriots formed a zealous, confident, and determined team in the field of evangelism, planting and writing several epistles. This constitutes a spiritual impetus for twenty-first believers in the area of Church planting especially in Regions that most need the gospel. Paul and his compatriots faced several daunting problems including persecution and false imprisonment. They used prayer to disentangle themselves from tyrants. In summary, the Book is a masterpiece and should be recommended to all believers, seminarians, biblical expositors, scholars, and Church planters to passionately read it and draw good lessons from it.

## BIOGRAPHY OF DOMINIC ADUA A. NYAABA, PH.D.

I was born in the year 1966 in Tamale, Ghana, and earned a Bachelor of Arts from the University of Ghana in June 1998, with a combined major in French and Linguistics, obtaining second Class honors. I received master of Divinity Degree in 2006 from International Theological Seminary, Los Angeles, California. In

June 2012, I earned my Ph.D degree from Newburgh Theological Seminary, Newburgh, Indiana. Currently, I am the Founder of Winning Life Theological Seminary in Los Angeles, California, the Founder of Winning Life Prayer Ministry, Los Angeles, California, the Founder of **Winning Life Security**, Los Angeles, California, and the Founder of Winning Life Schools and Tutoring, Los Angeles, California.

Furthermore, I received my academic and ministry Training from Catholic Missionaries, Presbyterian theologians, American, British, Canadian, and Dutch missionaries. I also worked as **linguist** for Ghana Institute of Linguistics, Literacy and Bible Translation. Prior to working for the Bible Translation Organization, I worked as High School Economics Teacher as well as High School English Teacher. Having succeeded in functioning with missionaries and different circular companies and Establishments, I have a wealth of experience in functioning with people of diverse cultures. I am expertise in the reformed and Wesleyan tradition, since I earned my Master of Divinity from reformed seminary, International Theological Seminary where I related with people of diverse cultural and racial backgrounds. I also have enormous knowledge in **Evangelical theology** and tradition since I earned my Ph.D in Biblical Studies from an evangelical Seminary whose academic philosophy is high reasoning and high-level academic impetus.

Pertaining to academic and seminar paper presentation, I have an immense experience in seminars and research paper performance. At Ghana institute of Linguistics, Literacy and Bible Translation where I worked as **Linguist**, from 1999-2003, I was the seminar organizer, and presented research papers ranging from **morphology, phonology, grammar,** and cultural traditions of designated speech communities. Some of these research papers were published to enhance the research aspect of the Organization. In a similar dimension, during the course of my theological and academic endeavors, I presented several papers in class for fellow students and professors to critique my findings. I scored grade **A+** in all seminar and research papers exhibited in seminars. At the Ph.D.

program, I employed all research tools, leading to the production of a masterpiece of **Dissertation** titled, *The Kingdom of God and Its Implication to 21ˢᵗ Century Believers.* I administered questionnaires in the area of contemporary, ethical and moral issues confronting believers in the kingdom of God in the 21ˢᵗ Century. The results were startling, spectacular and academically centered. Thus, I am prepared in the academic domain, ministry endeavors, leadership and spiritual dimension to lead 21ˢᵗ Century youth and adults to achieve academic laurels in the various theological programs offered at www.winninglifeprayerministry.com.

I have massive knowledge and experience in Tertiary Education since 2010. I am the founder and professor of Winning Life Theological seminary where I offer cutting-edge **online** theological programs. Since 2007, I have contributed colossally to the academic advancement of students in Los Angeles County by teaching and tutoring them in English Language Arts and Algebra. I prepare student to take California High School Exit Exams (CAHSEE), and SAT (Scholastic aptitude Testing). I am a man of honor, vivaciousness, love, intelligence, accommodating, full of wisdom, very mature, dependable, awesome, trustworthy, and abides by the laws of the Land.

I am the Senior Pastor of Winning Life Prayer Ministry. I am the president and Board Chairman of Winning Life Theological Seminary/Winning Life Prayer Ministry. Before the inception of Winning Life Theological Seminary and Winning Life Prayer Ministry, I was the Sunday school superintendent and Associate pastor of **All Souls Christian Center** in Los Angeles, California. I was a visiting preacher to **Labor For Christ** in Los Angeles, California. I was the associate pastor of Fountain Gate Chapel, Tamale Branch, where God used me to perform miracles in Healing and deliverance. I also worked as Associate pastor of Fountain Gate chapel in Ouagadougou, Burkina Faso where I preached the word of God and helped established the Church firmly in Christ. I was a school prefect, house prefect, secretary of **Northern students Union,** University of Ghana Division. I have over the years participated in

Board and Leadership meetings. I am academician, a theologian and wield intellectual power to lead Winning Life Prayer Ministry to unlock peoples' 21ˢᵗ Century destinies. Leadership dexterity leads to provision of abundance of mental, spiritual, psychological, financial, social, political and academic prosperity. I am well trained to handle finances of Winning Life Theological Seminary and any business organization. I am an excellent and well-trained business executive. I am trustworthy and have the fortitude to strive and triumph in my career as faculty, teacher, theologian, educator, pastor, teacher and preacher of the word (*logos and rhema)* of God.

## ACADEMIC RESUME/ CURRICULUM VITAE

- Ph.D. Newburgh Theological Seminary, Newburgh, Indiana, 2012 (Biblical Studies, exegesis, interpretation, Book Reports, Ethical issues, Church History, Evangelism, Apologetics, Prolegomena, Contemporary social issues, Doctrine of God and man, New and Old Testament Studies, pastoral Theology, Christian Education, prophets, Isaiah, Jeremiah and minor prophets, Greek, Hebrew, Research and Dissertation)

- Masters of Divinity, International Theological Seminary, Los Angeles, California, 2006 (Graduate level Theology and Religion Courses, several term papers, ethical and contemporary issues, as well as research work). **NT Greek, Hebrew, Pentateuch, Homiletics, Counseling in Ministry, Bible College Administration, Pastoral Theology, Prophets, Calvin's Institutes, Research Methodology, Middler Preaching, Christ and Salvation, Evangelism, Missions, and Urban Ministry, Psalms, Curriculum Development, Exegetical Methods, Doctrine of God and Man, Family Life Education, senior Preaching, Christian Ethics, Genesis 17, Church History, Isaiah, Jeremiah, and**

**many Theology courses.** Economics (Economic systems, economic planning and budgeting, Advanced Economics, Market systems, equilibrium price, Elasticity of demand, types of businesses, Supply, National income and gross domestic income computations, Income and expenditure, and a host of others.

- Graduate Certificate in Theological studies, Christian Service College, Kumasi, Ghana, 2001(General theology and Religious Studies). Major courses consist of Systematic Theology, New and Old Testament studies, Greek, Missiology and cultural studies, Islam, Buddhism, and African Traditional Religion.

- BA, University of Ghana, 1998- Major in French and English (Linguistics), **Second class honors**-(Main courses in Linguistics are morphology of English, Grammar of English, Syntax and Semantics of English, Phonetics, Phonological theory, Sociolinguistics, oral literature, Theory of Translation, Language and culture, Introduction to the nature of Language, and phonology of English). Main courses in French included **French usage, French dissertation, writing, and text based oral exercises, summary writing and essays, Functional French, Aspects of Francophone African Literature, Oral discussions and analysis, French novel up to Balzac, French thought, Aspects of Modern French Literature, and introduction to French Literature and text. Major courses in Islam consist of** the Prophet Mohammed, the Caliphates, Hijira, History of the Arabs in the Arabian peninsula, The Koran, Hadiths, the Bedouin Arabs, Arabic language studies, Islamic wars, Khadija, Fatima, Outman, Aboubakar, Omar, Ali, daily prayers, the call of Mohammed in the Arabian Desert, suphism, and many more Islamic Studies.

- Advanced Studies, Prempeh College, Kumasi, Ghana, 1990 (Major in French, Economics, and Geography)

- High School – St. Charles Secondary School (Minor Seminary), Tamale, Ghana, 1988 (Major in English Language, English Literature, French, Economics, Agriculture, History, Geography, and Math). Obtained first Division at the Ordinary level.

- Middle School- Salaga Roman Catholic Middle School, 1983 (Middle School Education)

- Elementary School- Kokofu and Kparigu Local Authority Primary Schools, Atebebu and East Mamprusi Districts, 1982(Elementary Education)

## CREDENTIALS

- **CSET-California Subject Examinations for Teachers.** In-depth study of **Literature and Textual analysis**, which involves **Literary Elements, Literary Criticism and non-literary Texts.** I wield the dexterity to read between the lines of a story, poem, play, historical document or essay passage and understand the author's thematic connotation. I have the ability to recognize, compare, and evaluate various literary traditions such as American cultural pluralism, British cultural pluralism, World literature (cross-cultural literature), Mythology and oral tradition. I have impeccable knowledge of the following: **Plot, setting, characters, point of view, Language, symbol, and theme, deductive and inductive reason, modernist poet, historicism, audience**

**and purpose, rhetorical jargon, syllogism, impressionism, imbiac pentameter, logos, pathos, ethos, topos.**

- I participated in the Field Test of the California Subject Examinations for Teachers (CSET) in English III Field Test, and English IV Field Test on March 8, 2014, and on March 18, 2014 organized by Pearson Education Inc. In the field Test, I examined rhetorical devices, literary devices used in poems, and texts. I identified significant themes that two texts shared. I compared and contrasted the writer's two perspectives on the theme I identified, and then I examined how the writer used literary techniques, including genre features, literary elements, and rhetorical devices to express his perspectives on this theme in each piece. Finally, I drew conclusion that explained how literary techniques identified in the texts affected the ideas conveyed in the texts.

- As trained Linguist, I wield the dexterity to delve into **morphology, inflections, Derivations, phonology, syntax,** (which is primarily concerned with the ways in which words are put together in sentences), **etymology,** which is the study of word origins and evolutions, and semantics, the meaning of words in a sentence. Furthermore, as a grammarian, I have the skill of teaching **noun phrases, subordinate clauses, verb complements, verb phrases, adjectival phrases, prepositional phrases, infinitival phrases, content and non-content nouns,** and I have been teaching English Language Arts for 20 years.

In addition, as a writer, I wield the communication abilities in both Written and verbal communications. I have been delivering speeches in Churches, and graduation ceremonies. I have published several articles in newspapers.

I have acquired the skill of responding to prompts, and have the creative ability to respond to creative *writing* prompts.

- I am a qualified teacher of English Language Arts, Math; algebra 1, and Algebra 2. I am a qualified teacher of Grammar and Morphology of English, English Comprehension, Literature, Types of Essays; narrative, expository, Argumentative, and Descriptive Essays. I am prepared to teach syntax of English. I am an expert in phrases, clauses, complex sentences, compound sentences, appositives, figurative language; simile, Metaphor, oxymoron, personification, hyperbole, textual analysis, parallelism, repetition, social linguistics, applied linguistics, Direct and indirect speeches, Direct and indirect object, anthropomorphism, and a host of others.

- California Basic Educational Skills Test (CBEST)- February 25th 2008, January 28, 2013. I exhibit excellent performance in writing, English Grammar and composition.

## Academic Courses and Certificates

Nyaaba, A.A. Dominic, 2001 "Syntax of African Languages." Conducted by Summer Institute of Linguistics, under the auspices of Ghana Institute of Linguistics, Literacy and Bible Translation, September 3-28, 2001, Ruiru, Kenya.

Nyaaba, A.A. Dominic, 2001, "Phonology of African Languages." Conducted by Summer Institute of Linguistics, under the auspices of Ghana Institute of Linguistics, Literacy and Bible Translation, October 30- November 22, 2001, Ruiru, Kenya.

Nyaaba, A.A. Dominic, 2001, "Introduction to Tone Analysis in African Languages." Conducted by Summer Institute of Linguistics, under the auspices of Ghana Institute of Linguistics, Literacy and Bible Translation, October 29-Novemebr 23, 2001, Ruiru, Kenya.

**Fields of Specialization:**

Biblical Theology (Exegesis and Interpretation)

Exegetical methods

Preaching (Expository, Thematic preaching)

Theological Studies, and Doctrine of God and man

Pneumatology (Study of the Holy Spirit)

Ecclesiology (Study of the Church)

Eschatology (study of Last things)

Historical Theology

Philosophical Theology

Pastoral Theology

Ministry and Counseling

Contemporary social problems and Christian Ethics

World Religions (Christianity, Judaism, Islam, Buddhism, Hinduism, African Traditional Religion)

Christian Apologetics and prolegomena

Evangelism, Missions and urban Ministry

Christian Education and Bible School Administration

**Elementary School, and High School English Grammar, Comprehension, and composition**

**Elementary School, Middle School, and High School Math (Algebra 1, Algebra II).** Commutative and Identity properties, Exponential notations, Associate properties, Distributive property of Multiplication, addition, Solving types of equations, integers, and number line,

Rational numbers, addition, subtraction, and multiplication of rational numbers, inequalities, multiplying and Dividing Monomials, Polynomials, linear equations, Graphing ordered pairs, Equations and slopes, areas, and perimeters of geometric figures, rational expressions, radical expressions, and many more. **French Grammar and Dissertation** and **Bachelor and High School Economics**

**RESEARCH INTERESTS**

- I am interested in Biblical Theology with special emphasis on Greek language, interpretation, research work, and exegetical methods

- Very interested in Economics issues, factors that affect national and international economics of scale, prosperity, business factors, and national income computations.

- Very interested in Ethical issues confronting 21st century Believers, using questionnaires, and philosophical projections to ascertain facts about Contemporary and ethical problems.

- Interested in General theological research including systematic theology, the Doctrine of God and Man, Holy Spirit, Church and Eschatology, Evangelism, apologetics,

Church History, New Testament and Old Testament Studies, and Philosophical theology as well as prolegomena.

- World religions such as Islam, Buddhism, Christianity, Catholicism, African Traditional Religion, Hinduism, Judaism, and a host of many other Religions of the world.

- I am interested in research that deals with etymological studies, and comparative Religions.

- I am interested in English Language; grammar, literary analysis and composition.

**Research and Academic Experience:**

2012- Ph.D. Dissertation project: **The Kingdom of God and its implication to 21st Century Believers (218 pages).** Statement of the problem, Goal and significance, Methodology focus, Literature review, formulation and administration of questionnaires, footnoting, single author and multiply authors footnoting, Ibid, quotations, paraphrasing, outstanding introduction, great chapter division, gathering of data, analysis and tabulation of data. In addition, employment of grammatically appropriate constructions; simple, complex, and compound sentences usage, avoidance of redundancies, tautology, and incomplete statements. Syntactically, and semantically appropriate use of ideas, and lexical items. Exegetical methods fittingly employed as well as Interpretation of complex and detailed evidence and use of quantitative data verbally and visually. Biblical Languages, Greek and Hebrew transliterated, and used in their apposite contexts. General citation practices, types of Bibliography style, as well as spelling, punctuation, and finally appendix: Paper formant and submission.

2006 –Master of Divinity program, Thesis: The Study of Genesis 17, Comparison of Biblical Marriage with Traditional Ghanaian Marriage

2004-2006- Research papers, Term papers, and essays at International Theological Seminary, Los Angeles, California.

2010- Present. Faculty, Professor, Bishop/pastor, Educator, Winning Life Prayer Ministry, Los Angeles, California

1999-2003- Linguistics Research. Ghana Institute of Linguistics, Literacy and Bible Translation

2003 I researched in Taln (Dialect of Gurene Language).

2003 I Researched in Gurma and north Guang languages.

2003 Researched in Gur languages.

1999 to 2002 I researched in the customs of the Kaakyis. I produced a graduate level research on Phonological Processes of the Kaakyi language.

1999 to 2003 I researched in Kaakyi Language; vowels, consonants, transcriptions, morphology and Phonology of Kaakyi.

1983-1998- French studies and Translation, University of Ghana, Prempeh College, and St. Charles secondary school, Ghana

**Book Reviews and Reports**

2012- *Encountering the Old Testament,* by Bill T. Arnold and Bryan E. Beyer (Biblical and exegetical approach to the interpretation of the Old Testament), Baker Academic, a division of Baker Publishing Group, 394 pages

2011- *Encountering the New Testament,* John Ashton (Biblical, and exegetical interpretation of the New Testament), Grand Rapids, Michigan: Baker Academic, a division of Baker Publishing Group, 384 pages

2011- *Thirty-days to understanding the Bible,* by Max Anders (Biblical Survey and interpretation of the entire Bible), Nashville, Tennessee: Thomas Nelson Inc., pages 299

2011- *The Religion of Paul the Apostle,* by John Ashton (Biblical, philosophical, and comparative approach to Pauline Theology), New Haven and London: Yale University Press, 300 pages

2011- *Encountering the Book of Psalms: A Literary and Theological Survey,* C. Hassell Bullock (Biblical and exegetical approach to the interpretation of Psalms), Grand Rapids, Michigan: Baker Academic, a division of Baker Publishing Group, 373 pages

2011-*The Jesus I never knew,* by Phillip Yancey (Biblical and Philosophical approach to Christology), Grand Rapids, Michigan: Zondervan, 288 pages.

2006- *Choosing the Good,* by Dennis P. Hollinger (Christian Ethics and philosophical approach to ethics), Baker Academic, a division of Baker Publishing Group, 272 pages

2006- *The Revelation of God: Contours of Christian Theology,* by Peter Jessen (Christian Theology), Downers Grove, Illinois: Intervarsity press, 285 pages

2006-*Preaching to the Postmodern World,* by Johnston Graham (Homiletics and Middler preaching), 253 pages

2004- *The Work of His Hands,* by Ken Gire (The Doctrine of God and Man), 220 pages

2004- *Beyond Accreditation: Value Commitments and Asian Seminaries,* by, Joyce Oyco Bunyi. International Theological Seminary (Christian Education), 310 pages

## TEACHING EXPEREINCE

2010-present: Professor of Theology, Winning Life Theological Seminary (Winning Life Prayer Ministry), Los Angeles, California and Ghana, Tamale. I am Professor of Associate Degree in Bible studies, Professor of Bachelor of Theology, Professor of Bachelor of Ministry, Professor of Bachelor of Biblical Studies, Professor of Bachelor of Counseling, Professor of Bachelor of Church History, and Professor of Bachelor of Pastoral Leadership. I am also outstanding Professor of Master of Theological studies, Professor of Master of Divinity, Professor of Master of Biblical Studies, Professor of Old Testament and New Testament studies, Professor of Master of Church History, and Professor of Master of pastoral Leadership. Research specialist and outstanding Professor of Doctor of Ministry (D.MIN), Professor of Doctor of Philosophy in Biblical Studies (PH.D), Professor of Doctor of Philosophy in Pastoral Leadership (PH.D), and Professor of Doctor of Theology (TH.D).

2007-Present: Academic Instructor of Winning Life Schools and Tutoring (Winning Life Prayer Ministry), WECAN Foundation and Say Yes To Life Tutoring services, AAA Academics Tutoring Services, 1 A1 Tutoria Computer Tablet Tutoring, 10401 suite 200, Venice Boulevard, Los Angeles, CA 90034, and **IPad and Android Computer Tablet** Tutoring 10401 suite 444, Venice Boulevard, Los Angeles, CA 90034. My primary function include the following: **students' assessments, students' registrations, writing of students' Learning plans, tutoring, and writing of progress notes, students report writing, and submission of bi-weekly timesheets. Students comprised mainly of grades 0 to 12. While providing educational support and services in the various school districts in Math and English Language, I also assist students preparing to take the California High School Exit Exam. Some are also assisted to prepare adequately for SAT. Content of tutoring include vocabulary acquisition, phrases, clauses, types of sentences, comprehension, textual analysis as well as teaching students to comprehend features of narrative, expository, descriptive, and argumentative letters. Students are also assisted to write such** letters. Content standards also comprise of phrasal verbs, finite and nonfinite verbs, regular and irregular verbs, the use of adjectives, adverbs, nouns and pronouns, types of sentences: simple, complex and compound sentences.

From grade1 through grade 3, I tutor students to develop mathematical skills and competence by learning to add, and subtract numbers 0 to 20. Our I help them to develop self-confidence and aptitude to solve problems like 2+4=6, 8+5=13, 12+7=19, and 10+10=20, and be able to subtract numbers within 20. I assist my students to subtract numbers within 20. For example, they know how to subtract 12-6=6, 17-10=7. I assist them to count up to 150. Grade two students are tutored to add and subtract numbers within 100, and using objects or bubbles to determine total number of objects in a Box. I also assist students to apply properties of operations to multiply numbers such as 3x 6=18, 8x2=16. In addition, from grade 4 through grade 12, I tutor students in **Operations and Algebraic Thinking, Number and operations in Base Ten, Number and operations=fractions, Measurement and Data, Geometry, Ratios and proportional Relationships, Number system, Expressions and Equations, Statistics and Probability, Number and Quantity, Algebra, Seeing Structure in Expression, Functions, Constructing viable Arguments, Reasoning with equations and inequalities, creating equations, monomials, binomials, and polynomials, Linear, Quadratic, and exponents, Vector and Matrix quantities.**

1999-2000, English Language (High School English Language), Advanced School of Accountancy and Management Studies

1984-1996, English and French teacher of children of professors of University of Ghana, and Ghana Institute of Management and Public Administration (GIMPA).

1991-1993, Economics teacher (High School Economics), St. Charles Secondary School, Tamale, Ghana. (Economic systems, Demand

and supply, International Trade, Factors of Industrialization, productivity, Division of Labor, the law of diminishing returns, Money and Banking, Per capita Income and National income computation, types of business organizations, Gross domestic product, stock exchange, bonds and securities, capital gains investment, Principles of economics, perfect markets, imperfect markets, input market structure, introduction to macroeconomics, introduction to microeconomics, introduction to national income accounting, inflation, consumer and theory, production and costs, general equilibrium and economic efficiency, and many others.

1990-1992 French Teacher, Nyohini Presbyterian Junior High School, Tamale, Ghana.

I taught **conjugation of verbs, introduction to French grammar comprising; the present tense, passé compose le future, le passé, plusque parfait, and French songs.**

# DOMINIC ADUA NYAABA, Ph.D.

Los Angeles, CA 90043 | 323-328-4518 |
winninglifetheory@gmail.com

Determined individual seeking an entry level Paralegal position in an environment where I may conduct legal business professionally and competently while collaborating with a diverse range of personnel including attorneys, associates, and clients. Along with my exceptional writing abilities and customer service skills, I will effectively assist with the ongoing success of a firm or legal team.

## EDUCATION

**Associates of Arts- Paralegal Studies** (ABA Approved) - *Current*
Fremont College, Cerritos, CA
Chancellor's Awards, GPA 4.00

**Doctor of Philosophy in Leadership**
Winning Life Prayer Ministry, Los Angeles, CA.
GPA 4.33

**Master's of Divinity- June 2006**
International Theological Seminary
El Monte, California and GPA 3.53

**Bachelor's of Arts in Linguistics and French**
University of Ghana
- Worked for Ghana Institute of Linguistics, Literacy and Translation. Developed Ghanaian languages using linguistic data.

**CBEST- Passed Writing (copy available)**
**CSET- Passed Trial Tests in English III & IV (copy available)**
*Teaching Credentials in process.*

## QUALIFICATIONS

- Legal Research And Writing
- Familiar with sources and priority of law in the U.S.
- Familiar with Civil Litigation preparation
- Gathering and organizing evidence
- Competent in completing Federal and State Judicial Forms, Cause of Action, Unlawful Detainer, Summons, and Process of Service
- Microsoft Word, Excel, Adobe, Internet
- Westlaw and ability to conduct research
- Experience and participation with mock trials, and court procedures
- Strong proofreading abilities, and attention to details

## PROFESSIONAL EXPERIENCE

**Faculty** - World Christian Theological University, Los Angeles, California.

**Faculty** - Winning Life Prayer Ministry.
- Owner of Winning Life Prayer Ministry, and approved by the Bureau for Post-Secondary Education to enroll students in various programs.
- Dean of Students, Winning Life Prayer Ministry.
- Provide Academic Programs and support for Winning Life Prayer Ministry.
- Focus on relevant students' resources and work directly with students to meet their academic and spiritual needs.

**Teacher- Uno A Uno Tutorials Companies, Culver City, CA**
- Registered students, and mentored them in English Language and Math.
- Taught and mentored students, assessed and made recommendations for further academia.
- Prepared and organized progress reports.

**Teacher- AAA Academic Tutoring, Culver City, CA**
- Driven and dedicated to assist students with studies, adjusting learning strategies as needed.
- Tutored and mentored students in various subjects.
- Assessed students on pretests and posttests scores and prepared progress reports.

**Substitute Teacher - New Design Charter School, Los Angeles, CA**
- Taught English and Math.
- Prepared and organized progress reports.
- Provided tools to help students improve academic performance.

**Winning Life Security – Owner - PPO number 18034 | PSE 634 - Los Angeles, CA**

- Private Patrol Operator, and Proprietor Private Security
- Licensed by the Bureau of Security and Investigative Services, undertakes contractual agreements for security work.
- Provide and protection services through Winning Life Security and liaising with the Police.
- Ensure the effectiveness and high-level standard services in security business.
- Highly professional and experienced security officer and PPO in Los Angeles.
- Obtained a security contract with Stratford school in 2016.
- Obtained an emergency security contract with Security Resources in 2015.

## VOLUNTEER EXPERIENCE

- Assisted neighbor with unlawful detainer in 2016, and case was successfully dismissed.
- Part of coalition that filed suit against the Los Angeles Housing Authority for negligence. Successful in obtaining order to relieve tenants of unwarranted rental payments through the REAP Program due to prolonged unaddressed repairs.

*Authorized to work in the U.S. for any employer*

# BIBLIOGRAPHY

Archbishop Dmitri Royster, *The Kingdom of God* [Crestwood, New York: St. Vladimir's Press, 1992], 26.

CCL.ORG (Accessed on July 2, 2014), 1

C. Hassell Bullock, *Encountering the Book of Psalms*, (Grand Rapids, Michigan: Baker Academic, 2001), 154-158

Centers for Disease Control and Prevention

Clowney, *The Messege of 1 Peter* (Downers Grove, Illinois: Intervarsity Press, 1988), 123. The imagery of a seeking shepherd illustrated in John 10:10:16, and Luke 15:5-7is attested in the Old Testament promise in Ezekial 34 where God condemns and judges the false shepherd for not seeking the lost (34: 6, 8) and promises to seek and gather his scattered sheep (34:11-13). The verb is used in active mood to describe turning to the Lord in Acts 11:21; I Thess.1:9.).

Dennis P. Hollinger, *Choosing the Good: Christian Ethics in a Complex World* (Grand Rapids, Michigan: Baker Academics, 2001), 127-138.

Eduard Schweizer, *The Good News According to Matthew* (Atlanta, Georgia: John Knox Press, 1975),339

Glen H. Stassen & David P. Gushee, *Kingdom of Ethics* (Downers Grove, Illinois: Intervarsity Press, 2003), 40

James Luther Mays, *Psalms, Interpretation: A Biblical Commentary for Teaching and Preaching* (Louisville Kentucky: John Knox Press, 1994), 116-119

Luis Berkhof, *Systematic Theology* (Grand Rapids, Michigan: William B. Eerdmans, 1996), 312- 313

Glen H. Stassen & David P. Gushee, *Kingdom Ethics* (Downers Grove, Illinois: Intervarsity Press, 2003), 41.

H.P Ruger A. Alt, O. Eibfeldt, P. Kahle ediderant, and R. Kittel eds, *Biblia Hebraica Stuttgartensia*: Stuttgarttensia, Vierte verbesserte Auflage, 1990], 1087.

Henry T. Mahan, *Bible Class Commentary, Hebrews and James* (England: Evangelical Press, 1984), 68, 84.

http://iandabasorihetr.hubpages.com/hub/7-Leadership-Characteristics-of-An-Eagle-That-Man-Should-Learn-From (Accessed on August 26,2013)

http://thealphanetworkeralliance.com/personal-development/you-must-possess-the-seven-leadership-characteristics-of-an-eagle/ (Accessed on August 26,2013)

Maxie D. Dunnam, *The Comentator's Commentary: Word Books,* (Texas:WACO, 1982) 212, 239, 241, 243-243.

Miles Van Pelt and Pratico D. Gary: *The Vocabulary Guide to Biblical Hebrew* (Grand Rapids, Michigan: Zondervan, 2003), 36.

Page H. Kelley, *Biblical Hebrew: An Introductory Grammar* (Grand Rapids, Michigan, William B. Eerdmans, 1992), 6.

Peter T. Obrian, *The Letter to the Ephesians* (Grand Rapids, Michigan: William B. Eerdmans, 1999), 46, 463-465.

Perry Downs, *Teaching for Spiritual Growth* (Michigan: Zondervan 1994), 17.

TBN, Santa Anna, California on November 8, 2012.

Thomas J. Stanley, *The Millionaire Mind* (Kansas City: Andrews Mcmeel Publishing, 2000), 52.

Robert H. Gundry, Matthew: *A Commentary on His Literary and Theological Art* (Grand Rapids, Michigan: William B. Eerdmans, 1982), 105.

Willard .H Taylor. *Beacon Bible expositions: Galatians and Ephesians* (Kansas City: Beacon Hill Press, 1982), 209, 212

William Barclay, *The letters to the Galatians and the Ephesians,* (Westminster Press 1976), 182, 183, 210-211.

*Young's Concise Commentary on the Holy Bible*, Robert Young, p. 180, 1977

Printed in the United States
By Bookmasters